# EARWORM

Eurovision and Gregory's Girl,
before and after.

One man's musical journey through life.

Colin Tully

Dedicated to Julia and my four daughters;
Nuala, Layla, Ailsa and Merryn.

# CONTENTS

# Acknowledgments

With thanks to Paul Karnowski for his painstaking copy-editing; Ailsa Tully for photo research; Carles Riba for formatting and pulling the whole project together.
7000 trees for the cover design.
Henry Shaftoe and Errol Walsh for reading it through and giving me positive feedback.

# Prelude

*'I have won several prizes as the world's slowest alto player as well as a special award in 1961 for quietness'*

*Paul Desmond*

I've been a musician all my life, teaching, composing and playing. A friend once commented that I'm more articulate musically than I am verbally. I feel inclined to agree with his observation. I mention this, not in a boastful way, rather as a statement of fact. After all, it could well be a negative thing to be more articulate musically than verbally, especially if you are a musician of very average skills.

A few years ago, scientists did some experiments where they scanned the brains of people as they listened to music. They discovered that very specific parts of the brain 'light up' with neural activity as the subjects listen to music. In a subsequent experiment they discovered that those same areas of the brain would register neural activity even when no music was being played and the subject was simply imagining the music, silently playing it through in their head.

These parts of my brain must be well 'lit up' as I have music going on in my head for the most part of my day; all manner of musical references, from snatches of songs to

1

imagined jazz solos. The above experiment made me realise that a lot of the time I am juggling two languages in my internal world, processing past events and planning future ones like I imagine most people do, but all the time with a music soundtrack playing.

Most people are familiar with the concept of an 'ear-worm', that annoying tune that you can't get out of your head. In my case I have what feels like a wormery of tunes, lined up like a playlist, accompanying me through the day's activities.

Some people are brought up bi-lingual with, for instance, a Welsh-speaking mother and an English-speaking father. In a way, I consider myself to have been brought up bi-lingually, having been from birth surrounded by the languages of both English and music. This may sound like a far-fetched statement; other people who are brought up in musical households would perhaps not make such a claim. However, I can only imagine that few young people are exposed to such a wide range of music as I was.

My family was not verbally inarticulate. We were not, however, a family of great storytellers. I cannot remember any long narrative yarns or political debates around the dinner table. It was music that was important to us. I think for my mother and father, the really important ideas, the transcendent, sublime ideas, were expressed through music.

In my childhood home I was, on a daily basis, exposed to music of all kinds, which, looking back seemed just as natural as listening to the spoken word.

Firstly, the bakelite wireless played its part.

I remember one time being in the car, the family in high spirits as we were on our way to Ardrossan to catch the ferry to Arran for our summer holiday. I had earlier heard a song on the wireless and to everyone's amusement I sang the chorus.

'Sugar in the morning,
Sugar in the evening,
Sugar at suppertime,
Be my little sugar, and love me all the time.'

Google tells me that the song was released in 1958 by the McGuire Sisters.

I was four at the time and had just discovered that singing was a way of earning smiles and attention from my family.

Around the age of five, my sister, Fiona and I would gather around the wireless on a Saturday morning to listen to 'Childrens' Favourites'. This was broadcast on the BBC Light programme from 9am.

For a couple of hours, we'd enjoy classics like Burl Ives' 'There was an Old Lady', 'Sparky's Magic Piano', Danny Kaye's 'The Ugly Duckling' and 'Billy Goats Gruff'. I was entranced, both with the images conjured up as well as with the melodies themselves.

But the music emanating from the Bakelite radio did not always appeal.

One evening, one of my brothers tuned into a programme of music which I had not heard before. I tried my best to like it but it seemed to me that there was no fun or joy in this music. To my young ears it seemed to be sung by sad and gruff old men with strange, twanging guitars that expressed pain and sadness. I left the room quickly, feeling uneasy. It was many years later before I discovered that I'd been listening to something called 'country music'.

I was the youngest of five siblings. My eldest brother, Graeme, was fifteen years my senior. Next in line was Brian, thirteen years my senior. Iain is ten years older than me, whilst my sister, Fiona, is some six years older.

Each member of my family contributed a different part to my musical education. Let me begin with Fiona.

I must have been around six or seven when Fiona and I began singing songs together. We probably spent more time singing together than we did talking. She taught me her own particular repertoire which she had picked up from the Guides and the Youth Fellowship at the church. We would typically have a singing session in the back of the family car, returning perhaps from a seaside trip down the Clyde coast. As I got older, and had been exposed to the harmony singing in my father's choir, I began to harmonise with Fiona's melodies. She was very encouraging.

Earlier, we sang children's songs like 'This Old Man' and 'There was an Old Lady' and, of course, the Glaswegian classic, 'Oh Ye Canny Shove yer Granny aff a Bus'. Once I was a little older and able to put in the harmony, we would sing songs like 'A Hundred Miles' by Peter, Paul and Mary or 'Blowing in The Wind' by Bob Dylan.

Richard Holloway came to our church as curate in the mid-sixties. He was a bright and charismatic young man, destined later to become Episcopalian Bishop of Edinburgh and later again, the celebrated agnostic author and broadcaster. He ran the Youth Fellowship group at St Ninian's. Richard had been in the USA and had picked up a range of what we called then 'Negro Spirituals'. He taught these to the young people at the church, including my sister, who in turn passed them on to me. Fiona and I therefore developed a whole new repertoire based on the spirituals. They were fresh and direct with syncopated phrases that pulled the melodies along. We sang 'Pharaoh's Army Got Drowned', 'You Gotta go Through That Door', 'Michael, Row the Boat Ashore', 'Hey, Sinner Man' and, of course, the song that everybody knew in the early sixties, 'Kumbaya'.

I remember watching Richard spontaneously leading a spiritual's singing session in the hall after church service one Sunday. People were washing up the plates and coffee cups and Richard, tea-towel in hand, was belting out a song which everyone had no choice but to follow. I was in awe. There was so much life in this music. I suppose something of the Afro-American experience came through and affected me, even in this second-hand rendition.

When I was nine, our parents took Fiona and me for an Easter break. Our brothers had by now outgrown the family holiday. We stayed at a farm house in the Ardnamurchan Peninsula, on the shores of Loch Sunart.

It was a long drive north from Glasgow, involving a ferry crossing across a loch at Ballachulish. Red deer allowed us to admire them by the roadside as we snaked our way along single-track roads into the Scottish wilderness. When we finally arrived, Fiona and I, having been cooped up in the Hillman Minx for so long, wanted to go exploring immediately. Behind our holiday farmhouse the fields rose up to meet heather-clad hills. Off we went, climbing up into the evening sky. Soon we were on top of our little world, among the glaciated contours of the Scottish mountains.

As if to celebrate, Fiona sang me the latest addition to her song repertoire, Peter and Gordon's 'World Without Love'.

'It was written by Paul McCartney' she enthused.

I was, by then, a Beatles fan and was suitably impressed.

'He's friends with Peter and Gordon' she continued. 'He wrote it for them'.

She taught me all the verses and together we sang at the tops of our voices knowing there was nobody but the wind to hear us.

'World Without Love' is a very trite and sentimental song. It is small wonder McCartney gave it to his friend, having considered it not good enough for the Beatles.

However, that really did not matter. As we sang, with the mountains all around us, it seemed as if Fiona and I had been transported temporarily to another spiritual plane. I had never before experienced freedom like this. It was as if we had found a new way to exist.

As we sprang back down the hill over the tussocks of heather, I think Fiona felt the same way.


It was Fiona who had introduced me to the Beatles. When they emerged onto the popular music scene in 1962, Fiona was thirteen, the perfect age for the Beatlemania frenzy that followed in their wake. She had managed to see them perform in Glasgow when they were on the cusp of becoming superstars and still under contract to tour around the provinces. She owned their early albums which she would play incessantly on her little Dansette record player.

Being much younger than Fiona, I would be sent to bed around eight o'clock. The compensation was that I could lie and listen as Fiona played side after side of her vinyl collection. She introduced me, in this way, to classic Beach Boys tracks like 'You're So Good To Me' and the sublime pop anthem 'God Only Knows'. She had many of The Kinks singles which she would play until the groove wore out. The LP, 'With The Beatles' was often played. I knew the sequence of songs so well on this album that when one track finished, I would know what the next one would be. I would lie in the dark, singing along in my head.

On the other side of Pollokshaws Road there was our local cinema, The Mayfair. It was here Fiona took me to see the two Beatle movies, 'Hard Day's Night' and 'Help'.

She also took me there to see Cliff Richard's 'Summer Holiday'. I think that, even then, I could sense that the approach of Cliff and The Shadows was a bit contrived, whereas the Beatles' songs were fresh and original. I was hooked on their music and loved each of their subsequent albums, 'Revolver', 'Rubber Soul' and 'Sgt. Pepper.'

My brother, Iain, had musical interests different from Fiona. I have no recollection of him going out and buying a 'single' or an 'LP' but all of us went to piano lessons from an early age and evolved different styles of playing.

I have an enduring memory of Iain sitting down at the piano in our lounge. I was around five at the time. He launched into something which I would now describe as boogie-woogie. The louche, driving propulsion of the left-hand pattern immediately made my ears prick up. He had only managed to play a few phrases when the door was flung open. In rushed my mother.

'Don't you dare play that!' she hollered, 'That's the Devil's music!' and taking the piano lid, she crashed it down.

I was astonished at my mother's outburst. Iain was, I think, amused that he had managed to annoy his mother so effectively.

Just as New York gangster rap has nowadays permeated youth culture across the globe so it was in the 1950s that rock 'n' roll had found its way across the Atlantic and became the language of teenage identity for my brother's generation in the west of Scotland. This was the sound that had the potential to sweep away all the fuddy-duddy, tightly buttoned-up culture of the past.

For my church-going mother it must have been a genuine worry that Iain was going to be led into life of depravity through exposure to music with such immoral overtones.

Iain had befriended a local lad, Colin Cunningham, who was a drummer in a band. One afternoon, Colin turned up with some of their friends and took over the lounge. Naturally curious, I went in to see what was going on. I was intrigued to see a snare drum on a stand. Colin was wielding drumsticks. The lads were all in high spirits and there was some talk of a 'jam session' about to happen. Colin set up a rhythm on the snare drum. Sadly, after a promising beginning, it fizzled out. I can imagine my mother must have had a word with Iain and nipped it in the bud.

I did however, receive my first drum lesson from Iain. One time, whilst waiting at table for our supper to arrive he picked up his knife and fork and played some rhythms on the table. I was quick to join in and we had a quick, cutlery-led jam session before our plates of food arrived.

One of Fiona's favourite singles was 'Funny How Love Can Be' by The Ivy League.

I have a memory of this song emanating from her bedroom doorway and Iain, with his chorister-trained voice adding a falsetto harmony to the chorus as he wandered through the hallway to his bedroom.

Brian was different again in his musical taste. Out of my three brothers he may have had the best singing voice. Somewhere in a drawer there is an acetate vinyl recording of Brian, with his dulcet treble voice, singing 'Sheep May Safely Graze' with the St Ninian's Choir, recorded before I was born.

Perhaps encouraged by this early recognition, Brian's musical interests turned towards singing. When I was little, I would hear him sing and play pop songs at the piano. He would pick up sheet music for popular songs from a shop in Pollokshaws Road. I remember him singing an obscure number, a gospel-flavoured spiritual, 'Old Man Mose is Dead'. He also sat at the piano and sang dreadful, sentimental ballads like 'Tammy's In Love' by Debbie Reynolds, the soundtrack to the 'Tammy' film series begun in 1957.

He later developed a craze for Connie Francis. Not often heard these days, Connie had a powerful voice and a series of hits with tracks like 'Lipstick On Your Collar' and 'I Want a Robot Man'. Brian had at least two Connie Francis LP's and seemed to play them relentlessly. Whether he fancied Connie Francis or just liked her blend of catchy 'Country meets Rockabilly' tunes, I'll never know.

Fortunately for us all, Brian outgrew his Connie Francis fascination and discovered, like nearly everybody in his generation, The Beatles.

Brian had an American pen-pal, Caroline, with whom he corresponded for a couple of years. Caroline came to Scotland for a holiday in the summer of 1963. Brian brought Caroline down to Primrose Cottage in Whiting Bay in the Isle of Arran where the family were taking their summer holiday. I can remember Brian, wild with excitement, doing the 'Twist' with Caroline in the living room of the cottage to the Beatles version of 'Twist and Shout'. Even though they were listening to the song on a transistor radio with tiny speakers, the energy of the tune was irresistible. The Beatles classic version, famously sung by John Lennon when he had a sore throat, had the nation's youth twisting their way to sexual revolution. I watched, as did Caroline, mesmerised, as Brian gyrated his pelvis. I hope he was not giving the wrong message to Caroline. Brian had decided, after spending a week in her company, that she was definitely not the girl of his dreams. The poor girl was probably totally confused.

Brian left school at sixteen and worked in John Smiths bookshop in Glasgow centre. With his new, expendable income he would purchase and bring home LP records. Alongside the Beatles album, Revolver, I can remember him playing well known classical pieces like Beethoven's Eroica Symphony and Schubert's piano quintet 'The Trout'. Now that he had turned his back on Connie Francis, he became more experimental in his taste.

One album he came home with was a recording of the Bartok String Quartets. This is not the easiest of listening, but for some reason I became fascinated with Bartok's eerie soundscapes and his use of wild Hungarian folk rhythms. Another album he bought, which I still love and occasionally play today, is an album of Greek Bouzouki Music. Traditional Greek music is a unique melting pot of European and Islamic influences and I was entranced by the virtuosic bouzouki playing on this album.

I temporarily gave up the piano around the age of twelve, having decided it just was not cool anymore. This, no doubt, was connected with the time a boy in my class saw me walking to my piano lesson and laughed at me. I was obviously a bit short on will power.

However, it was Brian's album of Teleman flute concertos that pointed me in another direction. I loved the liquid tones of the flautist on this album as he soared gracefully through Teleman's beautifully composed suites. After this epiphany, I nagged my parents to buy me a flute, who, seeing I was genuinely serious, finally gave in.

Brian's final contribution to my musical upbringing was his copy of Rodrigo's 'Concerto D'Aranjuez'. This version had the late, great Julian Bream playing the guitar part. With his sparse but beautifully placed orchestrations of Spanish and Moorish themes it is one of the great works of the last century. I remember playing it on my father's record player and being surprised to find my chest aching with the intensity of sadness which Rodrigo poured into the middle movement. At last, a piece of classical music was, as my mother would put it, 'sending me'. No wonder Miles Davis and Gil Evans had used Rodrigo's theme as the basis for their classic work, 'Sketches of Spain'.

Graeme was the jazz fan of the family. He developed a fluid 'soft -jazz' touch at the piano and learned several pieces by heart. He was influenced among others, by the gentle swinging approach of blind jazz pianist, George Shearing.

Graeme's one-time German girlfriend, Inge, gave him a jazz tutor book entitled 'Jazzklavierschule' and he learned a few pieces from this in the Jazz 'Cool School' style.

Nowadays, fifty years later, when I do a piano gig, I still play some of these pieces along with another of his favourites, Jerome Kern's 'Just the Way You Look Tonight'. Call me sentimental, but I like to think he is listening in.

Graeme brought a few records into the household.

There was a disc with Andre Previn playing jazz piano. However, the one that I loved and often played in my teenage years was a recording of the Modern Jazz Quartet.

Because J.S. Bach was played often by various members of the family, especially my father, I was very familiar with his style. On hearing the MJQ I immediately felt an affinity with their music as they were trying to combine Bach's contrapuntal approach with the freedom of jazz improvisation. I do not think my father approved of them, but to me the Modern Jazz Quartet seemed to make Bach's sound come 'up to date'.

The Swingle Singers were very much singing from the same hymn sheet as the Modern Jazz Quartet, in as much as they were re-inventing baroque music by making it swing.

Graeme had a couple of their discs. Some of the Bach pieces they sang were already familiar to us. To hear them sung so neatly, with that cool jazz rhythm section propelling the melodies forward, took Bach's music into another whole new level of possibility.

Of course, Graeme liked the Beatles too. I can remember visiting him and his wife, Hilda, in their new flat in Brenfield Avenue in Muirend. The décor of the flat was a revelation. It was so unlike the prevailing dark tones that I was used to back home in Tantallon Road. Here everything was light and modern. Contemporary-designed chairs and tables rested on Hessian square matting.

Graeme played me a track from 'Rubber Soul'. As I sat in Graeme's fresh and bright new living room my head took a turn. 'Norwegian Wood', with George Harrison playing the opening theme on a strangely exotic instrument which I would later identify as the sitar, in combination with these bright new surroundings gave me a sense that a whole new era was beginning, brimming with possibilities.

My mother I think was a frustrated musician. She had received piano lessons from an early age and had reached a reasonable standard of playing ability. The responsibilities of raising five children now meant that she had precious little time to develop her piano playing. Very occasionally she would take a few minutes out from her daily chores and go through to the piano in the lounge. She played in a rather faltering way as she was so out of practice.

She liked romantic pieces by the likes of Chopin and practiced up his famous Prelude in E minor.

When I was very small, I was a right little chauvinist. I became a bit puzzled or even resentful when my mother played the piano. I was not sure if I liked her in this role and wanted her back in the kitchen doing the ironing or preparing food like a proper mother.

She was very sensitive to music and responded more expressively to it than anyone else in the family. She, in this indirect way, taught me there was a transformative power in music that could help you transcend the daily grind and be uplifted to a different mental level. With her seemingly endless list of domestic responsibilities, she, out of us all, was in the best position to appreciate this. On occasion, listening to my father playing a piece of Schubert or Chopin, she would look up from her endless piles of ironing, look at me intently and enquire with a heartfelt sigh, 'isn't that music just sublime? Or, on other occasions, 'doesn't that music just send you?' At the age of seven I was a bit puzzled as to where the music was 'sending her'. It took me a few more years of living before I could appreciate just exactly what she was talking about.

Both my mother and father were 'old school'. They could not comprehend or relate to the 'beat' music coming out of the wireless or record player. It did not, to their ears, even qualify as music. Consequently, there was a generational divide. However, apart from the incident when my mother condemned Iain's boogie-woogie piano playing, my parents were generally tolerant of the popular music being played in the house. After all, there were five of us and only two of them so they had to accept it.

The only popular song that my mother seemed to connect with was 'Where Have All the Flowers Gone?' which I think she felt had some purpose and integrity. Written by Pete Seeger in 1955, it was popularised by Peter, Paul and Mary in 1961. It was a song which grew out of the protest movement and became associated with the Campaign for Nuclear Disarmament. Although it very much represented the spirit of the late fifties and early sixties for my mother it brought back the memories of the huge loss of young men's lives in the two world wars.

Having gone to sleep with Beatles songs in my head I would often wake to the sound of my father playing the piano. Part of his morning ritual would sometimes include playing a piece by Bach. He once told me it was his way of 'washing his brain', clearing his mind for the day ahead. He had memorised several pieces from the French Suites and the Two-Part Inventions, music he had been playing since his teenage years.

In the evening or at the weekend he might play something more romantic, perhaps something from Schumann's 'Album For The Young' or Schubert's 'Lilac Time'.

He loved Chopin and would entertain my mother toiling in the kitchen as his Ballades and Nocturnes resonated through our flat.

Although my father had been exposed to classical piano music and the musical traditions of the cathedral from an early age, he was by no means a musical snob. He had memorised an eclectic range of tunes in a lighter vein, pieces which were, I suppose, the pop music of his younger years. These were pieces from 1920s and 30s musicals, interspersed with folk tunes like 'Bee Baw Babbity' 'The Fairy Dance', 'My Darling Clementine' or 'Danny Boy'.

My father had two professions; company representative and musician. A proportion of his income, albeit a small one, was from playing the organ. He was given a small salary for his post as organist and choirmaster at St Ninian's. He also made money from playing at weddings and funerals in the church.

Around the age of six I was deemed old enough to join his choir. The choirboys rehearsed from 6.30 for an hour on Monday nights. We gathered in the little choir room at St Ninian's. Sitting on low wooden benches, we choirboys, perhaps twelve of us, would be put through our paces by our choirmaster. Looking back, it seemed that when my father entered into his role of choirmaster, he temporarily ceased to be my father. He certainly treated me just the same as the other boys which was a good thing, I suppose.

He would sit at the piano and, as a 'warm-up', exhort us to sing up and down the scales. Higher and higher we would go, gently stretching our vocal muscles.

Then we would practise the hymn, psalm and anthem for the forthcoming service on the Sunday.

On Wednesdays, we boys would again meet at 6.30 but would later be joined by the adult members of the choir; the altos, tenors and basses.

I can only look back from the distance of my current age and experience and say what a truly privileged experience it was to sing in that choir. To have my ears bathed in all these beautiful harmonies was a rich experience which laid the foundation of my musicianship.

My father was ambitious and wanted a high standard from us. We sang music ranging from the Elizabethan composers, William Byrd and Thomas Tallis, through the centuries, up to what was contemporary at the time, pieces which were quite challenging to sing. Once a year, we would take part in a choral festival where hundreds of choristers would come together to sing.

At the time, I took all this singing for granted, just part of the fabric of my life. Only later on did I realise how exceptional it had been. At fourteen, with adolescence kicking in, I rejected it, feeling embarrassed to turn up at church on a Sunday to wear flowing robes.

It was around this time that my father made an attempt to spark off in me an interest to learn the church organ. None of his sons had so far followed in his footsteps to become musicians so I must have been his last hope. He invited me down to St Ninians on a Saturday afternoon to have a go and see whether I would take to it.

The organ was tucked away, to the right of the chancel. I had looked inside this room from the choir stalls before but had never ventured in. It was my father's private domain where he had played the music for countless services over the previous twenty years.

As I placed myself next to my father on the smoothly-worn wooden organ bench, I felt like a novice pilot, sitting in the cockpit of a large plane for the first time. In front of me were the two manuals, or keyboards. On either side were rows of knobs, known as stops, with the exotic-sounding names of the various tones and pipes, printed under an enamel glaze. Below, lay the pedal board, a foot-size version of a piano keyboard.

To whet my appetite, my father gave me a demonstration.

He placed a well-used copy of Bach's Tocatta and Fugue in front of him, pulled out a few stops and proceeded to play.

I was temporarily won over. As my father poured his considerable skill into Bach's timeless masterpiece I could see and experience, at first hand, the dynamic power of the organ as it reverberated across the chancel from the pipes. Yes, I thought, I would really like to have a go at this.

Over the next few weeks, I had a few practices on the organ with my father showing me the various combinations of the stops and use of the two manuals. As time went on, however, I became defeated by the enormity of the project. I just did not have my father's skills at the keyboard and to acquire those seemed to be a very uphill struggle.

Also, in the back of mind, I felt that the church organ belonged to an older time and I wanted to connect with what was happening in my generation.

Besides, how could I resist the other musical stimuli coming through the airwaves which were pulling me in another direction?

There is a condition known as synesthesia. With this condition sensations derived from one sense pathway, eg sight or hearing can also be sensed and processed by a secondary pathway. With synesthesia, you might experience sound as a colour, or perhaps something that you see, as a taste. It was something of this phenomenon that I experienced one summer in Arran.

We were staying in Whiting Bay and being a beautiful sunny day, I had decided to take myself for a walk to Kings Cross. My route took me past some houses on the edge of the village. The heat was shimmering off the road and gardens were alive with colour and the heady perfumes of high summer. As I walked along some music drifted to me over a garden wall. I stopped in my tracks. Courtesy of someone's radio I was listening, for the first time, to the jingle-jangle, twelve-string guitar phrase from The Byrds 'Mr. Tambourine Man'.

To me, the sound of the phrase was so evocative that felt I was seeing the notes in colour. Then, when I heard the sweetly yearning harmonies of the chorus it felt I was experiencing the most profound moment of my life. To my young, naive ears it was as if the distillation of pure love was in those notes. Whatever it was, hearing that song made me want to be part of where it had come from.

For the majority of us the most obvious effect of the hippy 'revolution' was in how it influenced the popular music of the time. From the Beatles 'All You Need is Love' to the Beach Boys, with their hippy anthem 'Good Vibrations', the pop songs of the day had become spiritualised. Of course, some people simply jumped on the bandwagon, epitomised by groups like 'The Flower Pot Men' singing the very dire 'Let's go to San Francisco, where the flowers grow so very high'. But when John Lennon sang 'All You Need is Love' you did feel we were on a brink of a revolution in consciousness, and perhaps there really would be no more world wars.

With all this going on in pop culture it was small wonder I began to turn my back on the musical traditions of my parents. By the time I was in my teens I felt compelled to give up piano and choir and 'do' music in my own way.

First, I got the penny whistle. Then a guitar became essential if you wanted to convey a cool image to your school friends, so I got myself one and started picking and strumming folk tunes.

Then the whistle was upgraded to a flute. When I joined my first band around the age of fifteen my band mates thought the flute was cool, but could I play the sax as well?

I happily obliged and bought my first and only alto saxophone from my flute teacher's brother for sixty pounds. This saxophone, a 1932, Selmer 'Cigarcutter', has been with me all my playing life so far and will probably see me out.

Graeme encouraged me with the saxophone by buying me an album by the great alto saxophonist, Paul Desmond.

'You should try to develop a sound like that' he nodded towards the Dansette as I played the album for the first time.

In my dreams, I thought.

# EARWORM

## 1 The Summer of Love

*'When you play music, you discover a part of yourself that you never knew existed'*

*Bill Evans, pianist*

It's my second year at Hutcheson's Boys Grammar School and I'm in the classroom of Mr. Wilson, our gravel-chested German language teacher. He has just left us with instructions to learn a new vocabulary list whilst he sneaks off to the staff room for his customary ten-minute fag break. Of course, we've no intention of swotting up the list. Jim, Bill Crombie, a lad nick-named 'Cream' and myself are discussing a more pressing matter; what are going to call our new group? We scribble down names on pieces of paper and pass them around. After some debate we make our decision: 'The Pink Appetite'. It's suitably colourful, with psychedelic overtones in tune with the times.

A few days later we travel to Bill's house for our first practice. There is a piano there. I sit down and play the one chord sequence I've so far taught myself. Jim picks a few notes on his guitar but finds my piano playing tricky to follow. Cream, our lead singer looks around awkwardly. He was expecting to sing some pop song currently in the charts. Bill has no designated role in our group, perhaps on account of him being unable to play anything. Embarrassed he fills the hiatus by suggesting that maybe we could all go camping together. It's with some relief we drop the music thing and follow up Bill's suggestion. The Cairngorms would be good, somebody suggests.

So ends my first band rehearsal. The Pink Appetite seemingly don't have much appetite, well maybe only for the adventure of going on a camping trip.

It's lunchtime on Monday in our form room and after devouring our packed lunches Kenny Taylor is now holding court. Kenny is a lively lad who first came to my attention back in Primary School when some joker placed a drawing pin on his chair. Back then, Kenny delighted the whole class by melodramatically leaping off his chair and falling onto the floor with a good-natured grin all over his face. Even our teacher, Mr Terris, had been amused by his antics. Now Kenny is recounting enthusiastically to a small entourage the exciting event of his weekend. He has been to hear a rock group by the name of Pink Floyd in Glasgow's town centre. Kenny has crossed a new threshold. He is now an initiate into a new world of possibility, and we, the uninitiated, listen respectfully as Kenny describes how Pink Floyd do not just use an ordinary stereo PA system but have four speakers placed around the auditorium to create what is called 'quadraphonic sound'. We try to take it all in. The world of rock concerts and sound systems is all new to us and Kenny, as the first to venture out into this scene is ahead of the game. We listen as he goes on to describe the support act, the surreal Glaswegian performance poet, Ivor Cutler.

'There was this guy on before Pink Floyd, Ivor Cutler. He was doing really weird things. All these strange poems. At one point he pulled some socks out of his pocket and dangled them on the microphone stand." Two pairs of smelly socks, '' Ivor had proclaimed'. Kenny chuckles, still amused at the memory of it.

We adolescents were hungry for change and any cultural shifts going on outside of our very traditional education was music to our ears. Some of us were beginning to tune into the John Peel show on Radio 1. John played all the alternative stuff, 'underground,' as it was called, music that was too experimental to conform to popular tastes and therefore unlikely to enter the pop charts. However, there was one mainstream show on television that was still essential viewing for adolescents, namely, Top of the Pops.

It was ostensibly a show dedicated to the songs and bands who were most popular on one particular week, however in the sixties there was a revolution going on in musical culture and radical new artists, doing new and ground-breaking things, could find themselves selling thousands of records and earning themselves a place in the pop charts. TOTP was broadcast on Thursday evenings at 7.30 and on Friday mornings the chat at school was often centred on the performances we had seen the previous night. Jimi Hendrix, of course, astonished us, his tousled hair held loosely in a bandana, his hands teasing wild and unpredictable sounds from his electric guitar. I remember my father coming into the room one evening while TOTP was on. He watched for some thirty-seconds before declaring that it all looked like a 'lunatic asylum'. Jimi Hendrix was about as far away from my father's known musical world as you could get and it's hardly surprising, he could not relate to what was going on.

The 'Summer of Love' happened in 1967 causing sweeping changes in attitudes in young people. Young men started to grow their hair. The drab suits of the previous generation were being discarded in favour of jeans and garments made from fabrics normally associated with women, chenille, and velvet. Cheesecloth shirts from oriental markets were the thing to be seen in on warm summer days. Becoming aware of these alternative possibilities I began to resent my school uniform and what it represented.

Uniform was one thing but what was even worse was our school's policy on long hair. The school favoured the 'short back and sides' hairstyle of the previous generation and teachers, and especially the gym teachers vigorously opposed any attempt by boys to grow their hair long. If your hair had even begun to touch your ears you would be reprimanded and told to 'get it cut!' No doubt the fear amongst the staff was that long hair would lead to a lowering of moral standards, possibly ushering in an era of dope-smoking among pupils, falling exam results and, ultimately, a blighted image for the school. The school's long-standing reputation for excellence in education, some 300 years old, could not afford to be tarnished.

It is after a particularly short clipping from my Italian barber in Skirving Street that I take some desperate action. I gaze forlornly at myself in the mirror when I get home, looking with horror at the white patches of skin above my ears where the barber has enthusiastically clipped back a month's worth of hair growth. Something has to be done to restore my nascent long-haired image. I can't possibly go into school the next day looking like this. The solution quickly takes hold in my imagination.

Hair pieces.

I get to work, cutting out two curving pieces of paper. I then cut off some hair from a more hirsute area of my scalp and carefully glue the hair onto the bits of paper. With a bit more glue I stick the 'hairpieces' onto the offending bald patches above my ears and, hey presto, I am once more a vision of coolness.

Image restored, I saunter into school the next day, confident in my long-haired look. I actually get away with it for a few days before I get rumbled. In classes, we are arranged in rows and a lad sitting behind me, Iain Muir, has the perfect opportunity to view the back of my head. The earpieces are quite convincing from the front, but not so from the back. In our form room at lunch time Iain makes the announcement. 'Hey, everybody. Tully's got earpieces!' Iain's fingers have already pulled one off and he holds it aloft for all present to see. Strangely, I do not experience humiliation but rather sense a wave of appreciation for my cunning plan to outwit the short hair ban.

In 1967, The Beatles released their most ambitious album to date, 'Sgt Pepper's Lonely Hearts Club Band'. It was my brother, Brian, who bought a copy. For several weeks it was the favourite on our Dansette turntable. It was an album that not only displayed the unerring charm of the Beatles' song- writing skills but also their flair for innovation. In their early recording days, they had come into the studio to record a whole album of sixteen songs in just a couple of days. Now the studio had become an experimental laboratory where they would spend weeks trying out new ideas in sound production and recording techniques. They too had been affected by the social revolution going on in 1967, had embraced transcendental meditation in India, and also taken a fair amount of the consciousness-changing drug, LSD.

The album's psychedelic qualities had a profound effect on me. I was hypnotised by the shimmering guitar arpeggios in 'Lucy in the Sky with Diamonds', haunted by the exotic Indian instrumentation of 'Within You and Without You'. The desire to repaint my bedroom, I think, was a direct response to listening to Sgt Pepper. Somehow the technicolour imaginings of The Beatles made me want to make my bedroom a more colourful place.

Home decorating was a regular feature of family life and my help was sometimes enlisted by my parents to help them paper a wall or paint a skirting board, so I had the necessary skills. I decided to paint my walls two different colours, turquoise and mandarin orange. I can still recall the smell of the paint as I splashed away with my paintbrush, with Sgt Pepper egging me on from the turntable. I was pleased with the result. Sure, I still had to go to a school which forbad long hair and I still had to wear a boring uniform, but now at least, I had the deep satisfaction that my true self was expressed on the walls of my bedroom.

In second year of secondary school, I began to hang out with Jim. Jim was a gentle mellow lad who was easy company. I spotted him one day with an LP vinyl tucked under his arm. This was an album, ironically named 'Mr.

Wonderful' by Fleetwood Mac, the front cover being a full-size photo of Mick Fleetwood displaying his scrawny naked torso underneath a hat and a mischievous grin. This version of Fleetwood Mac was not the Anglo-American super-group, but it's purely British precursor. Their name was derived from the names of the founder members, John MacVie and Mick Fleetwood, bass player and drummer respectively. The group also boasted the talents of Christine Perfect (later McVie) on keys and the superb guitar playing of Peter Green. Jim invited me around to his flat on the other side of Queen's Park to have a listen. Essentially Fleetwood Mac were, at this point in time, a blues band, often emulating the blues style pioneered by Chicago based guitarist, Freddie King. I had at this point never heard of blues music. It was simple and direct and Green's solo guitar work was silky and seductive. Jim and I both had acoustic guitars and together we attempted to strum along to tracks like 'Dust my Broom' and 'Dr Brown', the sexual innuendo of the song lyrics flying way above our fourteen-year-old heads.

Going over to Jim's at the end of the school day began to be a regular occurrence. My first guitar was a primitive affair, steel-strung with an action that threatened to make your fingers bleed. I was prepared to overlook this issue such was my enthusiasm to learn all the chords and finger-picking styles on offer. Jim and I were both self-taught, learning from guitar tutor books such as those compiled by Mel Bay and John Pearse. We traded what we had learned from these books and began, with our limited technical knowledge, to write songs. Jim was a romantic soul and set poems to his arpeggiated guitar style. He even began to compose his own poetry. Inspired, I took up the challenge and attempted to write my own. I can now confess, all these years later, that I actually pinned these terrible attempts at poetry onto my newly painted turquoise and mandarin bedroom walls hoping to impress any friend who happened to come round. Jim, on the other hand, was way ahead of me in the lyric department and even managed to get a poem published in an 'alternative' magazine. It was a kind of protest poem which grumbled about the unnatural imposition of British Summer time and how shifting the hour twice a year interfered with his 'body-clock'. I can still remember the first two lines:

'I've still got cornflakes roaming around my tummy.

The dark morning, it's sunny'.


It was Jim who tipped me off about the Indian musicians coming to the McLellan Galleries in Sauchiehall Street. We both knew that George Harrison had dabbled with Indian music and played sitar on John Lennon's 'Norwegian Wood'. We'd also heard the Indian musicians on 'Within You and Without You' on Sgt Pepper, so we were curious to hear more.

What we hear is a full-on concert of classical Indian music with no pandering to Western sensibilities whatsoever. This is perhaps a little more than what two fourteen-year-old lads have bargained for. Initially, I remember being a little disappointed that Debabrata Chaudhuri is not playing the sitar. He is playing another long-necked, lute-like instrument called the sarod which, on hearing its exotic tones I quickly decide is a good substitute for my sitar expectations. On stage, Debabrata is joined by a tabla player and a young woman playing the Indian drone instrument, the tamboura.

Looking back, Jim and I did very well to listen patiently to what was a whole different cultural experience. Compared to the quick hook lines of western pop music that we were used to; Indian classical music could seem ponderous and uncompromising to the uninitiated. The musicians played several ragas, the standard musical form in India where the musicians improvise on a particular scale over a complex rhythmic cycle. Each raga started slowly with long sinuous phrases, demonstrating the subtle melodic phrasing of Indian improvised music. The sarod sang out with a clear alto tone. Once the tabla player joined in, the energy gathered momentum and the music built to an exciting climax when the musicians demonstrated a rhythmic and melodic interplay of breath-taking skill.

Jim and I come away from the performance uplifted and our horizons broadened. However, our musical tastes were nothing if not diverse, the next outing being our first live rock concert. This event took place entering from Glasgow's famous Sauchiehall Street. The managers of a large ballroom had in the late sixties caught up with the hippy revolution and had given the former dance hall a new name. 'The Electric Gardens'.

To attend our first rock concert at such a cool venue we had to have the right gear to wear. What were fashionable at this time were ex-military greatcoats. These could be purchased from Army and Navy stores. Jim and I acquired these preposterously heavy coats which were designed for a long winter in the trenches. We may have had school regulation haircuts but at least our coats would show that we were part of the alternative scene.

The atmosphere in The Electric Gardens can hardly be more different from the gentile Victorian elegance of the

McLellan Galleries. The old dance hall is dimly lit and through the gloom we make out a sea of people spread out on the floor with the stage beyond in the distance. There are no chairs and the audience sits around in sprawling groups. We lumber forward into the crowd, self-conscious and sweating in our ridiculous greatcoats and manage to find ourselves a piece of empty floor. We do not know it then but we are about to witness a slice of pop music history.

We see three bands that night. First up are a local warm-up act. They are good players and, looking back, must have been influenced by the same British Blues Revival movement that I have heard on Jim's Fleetwood Mac LP, Mr. Wonderful. The lead guitarist does a great version of a tune which I later identify to be a Freddie King number called 'The Stumble'. This is my first experience of amplified music with a classic bass, drums and guitar set-up. The long-haired lads on stage, probably some five or six years older than me, are exemplifying the lifestyle and image I'm beginning to yearn for.

Next onto stage bounces the pixie-like presence of Marc Bolan with his bongo-playing bandmate, Steve Peregrin-Took. They sit right at the front of the stage, cross-legged on cushions, and deliver Marc's quirky songs from the current Tyrannosaurus Rex album, 'Unicorn'. This is a couple of years before Marc goes electric and changes the band name to T. Rex. It is essentially an acoustic sound very much in tune with, or perhaps, contrived to be in tune with, the hippy ethos of the time. Steve Peregrin-Took has taken his name from a character in J.R.R. Tolkien's 'The Hobbit', a book which, along with 'The Lord of the Rings' has become something of an alternative hippy bible. He provides percussion and backing vocals behind Marc's nasal warblings, which, I think, at times sound very contrived. The tunes, however, are fresh, direct and catchy and they deliver a lively performance which goes down well with the crowd.

The final performance that evening couldn't have been more contrasting with the fairy-tale performance of Tyrannosaurus Rex. This is Black Sabbath, a midlands band who epitomise an emerging new music genre, Heavy Metal. Very loud and very hairy they pound out their repetitive rock riffs to the audience who sit mesmerised as Tony Iommi assails their ears with lightning speed guitar solos in between Ozzy Osbourne's anguished vocals.

Clutching the mic-stand, Ozzy belts out his depressing lament 'Paranoid'.

'Finished with my woman, 'cos she couldn't help me with my mind.

Can you help me, help me with my brain'.

All this hyped-up emotion seems very silly. Nevertheless, the pounding beat produced by Geezer Butler on bass and Bill Ward's drums is having a powerful effect on the audience. All around me I notice heads beginning to nod in time with the propulsive beat, long hair wafting rhythmically to and fro. This, I am later told, is 'getting into the music'. To not be affected by the music and shake our heads in this manner might look uncool to other members of the audience, so with all the intelligence of a pair of sheep, Jim and I join the herd, close our eyes and shake our heads. Unfortunately, our school regulation haircuts do not allow the possibility of much hair-swaying, but at least we are trying.

The evening at The Electric Gardens was another stepping stone towards the new self that was quietly developing inside of me. Somebody said that Elvis Presley single-handedly created the phenomenon of teenagers having a separate identity, a distinct phase where young people could have the indulgent time to think of how they wanted society to change. Rock and Roll was one medium in which that separateness could be expressed. Before Elvis, teenagers did not have that luxury of time. Between the pressures of poverty and world wars young people went straight from childhood into adulthood with little time to adapt. Boys were apprenticed at fourteen or fifteen, girls often went into domestic service. For many, marriage and the responsibility of parenthood followed soon after. I was perhaps lucky to be born at a point in history when I could take my time with the process of growing up, to have a good look around and enjoy the relative freedom of youth.

As this new teenage self was developing it became increasingly at odds with my secret life at the church. My membership of the church choir at St Ninian's became something I found increasingly embarrassing. What would my friends think if they knew that on Sundays, I became a choirboy and donned a cassock, surplice and frilly ruff? I assumed they would immediately disown me and therefore kept it a closely guarded secret.

My brothers and sister had all done their time in the choir, my eldest brother Graeme singing as a tenor until he 'retired' from the choir at the age of twenty-one. But times were changing. How was I going to forge a new identity as a long-haired musician and yet continue to be a choirboy? It just didn't fit. At fourteen my voice began to break and I saw my escape route. My father, the choirmaster, had other ideas. Of course, I could stay in the choir as an alto while my voice changed, he gently suggested. Then, I could join the other men as a tenor or bass. This fate I accepted for a while as my treble voice, over a period of time, cracked and wavered, but I knew that at some point I was going to have to make a big decision.

◆

# 2 Cheesecloth and Velvet

*'Never play anything the same way twice.'*

*Louis Armstrong*

The first year of secondary school had been a bit of a lonely affair but by the time I moved into second year I had cultivated a few friends to hang around with. My friendship with Jim was something new. Gavin, on the other hand I had known a long time.

Gavin started coming to the church around the age of nine, his father being a Yorkshireman who liked the Episcopalian form of worship and so went to St Ninians on Sundays. Gavin joined both the wolf cubs and the choir and so we had plenty opportunity to meet up and get to know each other. We had sleep-overs at each other's houses, events that ended up in us hurling our smelly socks and underwear at each other across the bedroom, much more fun than going to sleep.

Gavin also went to Hutchie and in second year we began to spend more time together. Like with Jim, it was music that was the common interest. Gavin had also got himself a guitar, this instrument for us all being the ultimate cool status symbol, something you imagined commanded respect when you strode into school with it under your arm. Again, Gavin was self-taught from tutor books and aspired to writing songs.

Yet another guitar-playing friend was Kenny, he of Pink Floyd concert fame. He too had a go at song-writing.

I'm out one day near Shawlands Cross and bump into Kenny with an album cradled under his arm. This is 'The Hangman's Beautiful Daughter' by The Incredible String Band. 'I've just bought it', Kenny proclaims. 'They're really good. I'll lend it to you in a while if you like'. I look at the back cover, a photo of the coolest-looking, dishevelled bunch of hippies imaginable. I'm intrigued.

A week or so later, Kenny, good as gold, lets me have the album for a few days. On first listening I find it all very strange, like nothing I'd ever heard before. I can now from my current standpoint see where the String Band's influences were coming from, but as a naive fourteen-year-old, their sound was new, fresh and exotic.

The ISB, Robin Williamson and Mike Heron were very much a phenomenon of the hippy era. You either loved them or you hated them. Mick Jagger and Robert Plant both admired them. Paul McCartney said that 'Hangman' was his favourite album of 1968. Long before 'world' music had been coined as a term the ISB were doing it. For a teenage boy in the west of Scotland it was a ticket to a wide range of music culture, all contained on the one disc. In this one album you can hear elements of calypso, Scottish folk music, Old Time American country, Elizabethan lute music, singing in a Sufic style and shades of Bob Dylan, this, all woven together with exotic instrumentation; sitar, harpsichord, pan pipes and sarangi, blending freely with the virtuosic guitar playing of Robin and Mike. Their lyrics were often dreamlike, meandering, conjuring up an intriguing array of vivid images. The songs' melodies effortlessly etched themselves into my memory. Fifty years later I can still recall much of ISB's music and sing their songs to myself on long car journeys, nostalgic anthems to my long-lost youth. Back then I literally could not stop playing Hangman and as soon as a side was finished, I'd flip it over. I became a hopeless addict. I wondered how Kenny could bear to lend this priceless gem to me after only owning it for only a week.

On the evening of the second day of having the album in my possession my parents announced that they had bought tickets to see the famous flautist, James Galway, who was performing at the Kelvin Hall. A great opportunity and normally I would have happily gone along to hear him play. However, by this point I was so immersed in the world of the Hangman's Beautiful Daughter I found the idea of leaving my bedroom and not being able listen to the ISB's beautiful, intriguing collection of eccentric songs for two hours almost heart-breaking. Of course, I did tag along with my parents and Mr Galway gave a great performance on his golden flute. He even played a virtuosic encore on a penny whistle which I thought was really cool. But on coming home after the concert I quickly placed the needle on 'Nightfall', the last track on 'Hangman' and once again crossed the portal into my newly discovered sound world.

It was another common interest that brought Kenny, Gavin, Jim and myself together around the age of fourteen;

J.R.R. Tolkien's 'Lord of the Rings'. For us, reading this massive tome was like a rite of passage, an initiation. For weeks, if not months, we were all reading this book. Like the status exuded by carrying a guitar, bringing out a battered, well-thumbed copy of Lord of the Rings from your schoolbag was definitely an equivalent statement of cool. And it wasn't enough to read the 1000 or so pages of the book just the once. To show real commitment to your desire to live in Middle Earth you read it two or three times in a row.

Perhaps preceding generations of teenage lads had similar infatuations with one particular book. Maybe when Walter Scott produced Ivanhoe, swarms of young people fantasised about living in the Middle Ages where they could pretend to be heroic knights of old. But the huge sweeping epic scale of Lord of the Rings was on another level from Scott's novel. Tolkien had created a whole new world, populated by semi-mythical beings, elves, dwarves and hobbits and had even gone to the trouble of inventing languages for these beings to speak. We now know that the story of the hobbits, leaving the peace and tranquillity of The Shire and enduring countless trials and hardships to eventually overcome the forces of darkness is a metaphor for the First World War.

It was Kenny that got us walking. He was a member of the Ornithological Society and as such was responsible for reporting bird sightings in an area to the south of Glasgow. Consequently, he was familiar with various walks in North Renfrewshire. One walk was to a landmark named Walls Hill Fort, the site of a former Iron Age fortified settlement.

One crisp but blue-skied winter's day we, that is, Gavin, Jim and myself join Kenny on this walk. Having taken the bus out to the Round Toll at Pollock Park we head up the Kennishead Road, past the infamous Nitshill Estate and on out into the open countryside. Once we leave the tarmac behind, we feel we are on an adventure. Somebody comments on some aspect of our favourite book, Lord of the Rings, and we are off. For a moment I, at least, feel like a member of Tolkien's Fellowship of the Ring, the band of elves, dwarves and humans that came come together to protect the ring-bearer Frodo, and his hobbit companions. With the images from the book so embossed on our minds from frequent reading it is easy to identify the Renfrewshire rural landscape as a piece of Middle Earth and to imagine we are on some heroic mission. From a distance we get our first sight of Walls Hill. The fort is, of course, long gone but the natural ramparts of the long flat hill upon which it once stood rises impressively above the farmland. In my imagination it morphs into the former site of Minas Tirith, legendary city of the Men of Gondor. No inhabitants of Middle Earth are there to greet us but on arrival at the former hill fort we are treated to a spectacular display of icicles, dangling dramatically where a stream in warmer weather would make its passage down the former fort's steep sides. The icicles, some two feet long, glisten in the low winter sun like the teeth of Smaug the dragon.

It wasn't long after I had been initiated into the musical world of the ISB through listening to Hangman that they simultaneously released not just one album, but two; 'The Wee Tam' and 'The Big Huge'. I rushed out to buy my own copy of Wee Tam, to buy both albums being beyond the budget of my pocket money. This new collection of songs didn't disappoint with its lyrics blending mysticism, whimsy and stream-of-consciousness style prose. The opening song proclaimed in its rousing chorus,

'Maya, maya.
All this world is but a play, be thou the joyful player'.

Not a bad sentiment if you can be at ease with the biblical language.

I pick up my guitar and work out the chords. The chorus is easy; just three chords. Next day I take my guitar into school. Where I find the confidence, I'm not sure but at lunchtime in my form room I find myself strumming these chords and singing the chorus from Maya to a few of my assembled classmates. It is nothing short of an epiphany to discover that I can perform in this way and win the approval of an audience. I like the inner confidence the experience provides. I am not sporty and am academically mediocre. Here at last I have found something that I feel I could get good at.

I had given up my piano lessons around the age of twelve. On hearing the ISB I bought myself a penny whistle, not a huge financial outlay, and began to tinker with that. Soon after, my brother, Brian brought a copy of Telemann flute sonatas into the house. On listening I became captivated with the liquid sound of the solo flautist. I decided that if I could play the penny whistle then surely it would be an easy step up to play the flute. I nagged my parents to buy me one and eventually my enthusiasm won them over.

A flute teacher had to be found. This turned out to be a gentle, middle-aged man by the name of Solly Banks. He lived locally and I began a routine of weekly lessons on Saturday mornings. I loved these lessons and made good progress over a couple of years. My favourite times were when I got good enough to keep up with Solly and play duets with him composed by the early nineteenth century composer, Kuhlau.

Around this time a new genre of music was emerging; progressive rock, or 'prog rock' as it quickly became known. Elements of classical or jazz were blended into the rock mix, often extending the 3-minute song formula that had been around since the fifties. This was the era of the concept album with bands like King Crimson, Greenslade, The Nice and Traffic writing imaginative lyrics over more adventurous musical structures. One such band was Jethro Tull, bizarrely named after the eighteenth-century agrarian pioneer.

This outfit was led by flautist and vocalist Ian Anderson. The very first 'single' I bought was Jethro Tull's 'Love Story', released in January 1968. I liked the rocky electric guitar riff that propelled the song along and was curious to hear Anderson playing folksy flute phrases in the breaks between verses. To hear the flute on a pop single was a rare thing at the time. Ian Anderson cunningly devised a powerful image for his band which simultaneously rendered them acceptable to the alternative scene and yet remaining commercially viable. Boggle-eyed under a shock of unruly curls, he would stand on one leg, intersecting his declamatory vocal style with breathy flute phrases reminiscent of the jazz musician, Roland Kirk.

It was an exciting moment when they appeared on TOTP with their most successful single, 'Living in the Past'. We were all talking about it next day in school. The song was an eclectic mix of styles, jazzy flute with a string section backing and in an ambitious time signature, 5/4, a time signature only previously heard in the pop charts in Dave Brubeck's classic, 'Take Five'. It was challenging to dance to, yet the TOTP teeny-boppers in the BBC studio gave it their best.

It is known amongst my friends that I am now playing the flute. It's an obvious and corny connection to make, Jethro Tull's flute playing with my surname. Overnight, I have a new nickname

'Jethro'. In the form room at lunchtime, I oblige my mates and seal my new reputation by getting the flute out its case, standing on one leg and playing the first phrases from 'Living in the Past'.

When we devoted fans heard that the Incredible String Band are going to be performing at The City Hall in Candleriggs there was no question of us not buying tickets for this potentially momentous occasion.

On the night of the concert Kenny, Jim, Gavin and myself arrive to find a queue has already formed outside the City Hall's entrance lobby. We join the bustling crowd of young, long-haired people; students, school pupils, workers, their daytime occupations thinly disguised by donning as much hippy attire as they could find in their wardrobes…kaftans, chenille jackets, velvet scarves, denim jackets, Afghan coats and cheap, imported Indian jewellery.

A car pulls up and, to the general astonishment and wonder of the crowd, our favourite high priests of hippydom, Robin and Mike, are suddenly amongst us. Clutching instrument cases and resplendent in their own 'way-ahead' flower-power finery they make their way through the entrance, their awestruck fans hardly believing their luck at getting so close to their idols.

We find our seats, a central position not too distant from the stage. The mood of the audience is one of joyful expectation, a congregation of supplicants about to receive a musical blessing. Our two heroes bounce onto stage, Robin seating himself on a chair with his guitar, Mike sitting down cross-legged on a cushion, his sitar before him. Whilst they casually adjust tunings on their instruments, Robin engages the crowd in light-hearted banter. Then comes their opening song 'Maya'.

I remember initially being a mixture of excited and disappointed as I listen. Sure, this was the real deal. But it doesn't sound like the recording that I've etched on my brain over the past few months. It takes me a few moments to accept that this was essentially 'folk' music and unlike the strict precision of classical music here there is freedom for the musicians to adapt and change the way they sing and perform their material. I begin to appreciate how this gives their songs a freshly-minted quality, almost like they are just making it all up as they sing.

Later in their set the lads are joined by their partners, Liquorice and Rose, who waft onto stage like a pair of gypsies in their long skirts and bare feet. Liquorice contributes backing harmonies with her thin flutey voice and adds the occasional delicate chime of finger cymbals whilst Rose supplies bottom-end to the ISB sound with her purposeful bass guitar lines. It's all very natural and unaffected, these four charismatic individuals like a happy family performing for us, as if from their living room. When they play upbeat numbers like 'Cousin Caterpillar' and 'Log Cabin Home in the Sky' there is no doubting the infectious joy pouring off the stage. If anything epitomised the spirit of the times, this being only a year after the 'summer of love', that optimistic vision that we could all live together in this new creative and colourful way, it was, for me, that evening in City Hall.

The last number finishes and we're on our feet to give our grateful applause. Next thing, Kenny is making his way along to the end of the row. I'm informed by Jim that he's on his way backstage. I'm astonished. Kenny is going to try to speak to these divine beings. As the audience files out, we hang around in the foyer, waiting for Kenny to re-emerge, and marvelling at his boldness. I just can't get it. How could someone in my year at school, only fifteen, someone who wears a uniform from Monday to Friday and doesn't even have long hair think he is worthy to go backstage and enter into the company of these gods of psychedelic folk? After some ten minutes or so Kenny is back with us. Nonchalantly, but without boast, he tells us that it had been no problem getting past security. Sure, he'd had a chat with Robin. He'd noticed a small scar on his cheek.

Between the ages of 14 and 15 my social life opened up even more. This was a time when news would spread amongst my classmates that a party was going to be happening. Sometimes it was a boy in my class who persuaded his parents to let him throw a party. Sometimes we heard of parties happening where the host was a friend of a friend, someone whom we'd never met. Undaunted, we'd show up anyway, saying we were a friend of 'so and so' and blag our way in. Before turning up at these parties someone had to run the gauntlet of the off-licence. The biggest boy, or the one whose voice had broken and was showing the beginnings of facial hair would be nominated. Most of the time he'd get away with it, the shop keeper turning a blind eye. Cider was the favourite for us young drinkers, a close cousin of apple juice and somehow therefore not so incriminating as beer.

Once inside all manner of delights awaited. A chance to hear someone else's record collection. Cider-fuelled jokes and banter in the kitchen. A chance to speak to some new girls. Coming from a single-sex school girls were still mysterious and unfamiliar to me. The etiquette around physical contact was a case of trial and error. With the wave of peer pressure from my male friends, along with the hormone-driven need for new experiences, an encounter more often ended in clumsy error.

While I was fumbling my way into teenage hedonistic pleasure, by contrast my parents at this time were going through a process of deepening their faith. The rector at St Ninian's, the saintly John Taylor, organised a small group of his congregation to go on spiritual retreats. Some monastery or convent would provide the accommodation and the participants would for a couple of days take a vow of silence, using the time for reflection and prayer. One such weekend was coming up and I began to hatch a plan.

It was just a fledgling notion when I shared it with a boy in my class. Bad idea. Once it was out in the open there was no going back. Tully was having a party. The momentum gathered. As the word got around there was no doubt that was, I enjoying my moments of being Mr. Popular. However, as the weekend approached alarm bells were beginning to ring as more and more people told me they were coming on Saturday night.

I didn't reveal my plan to my parents. All my brothers had by this time married and left the family home and it was the responsibility of my sister, Fiona to keep an eye on me. I must have told her I was having a few friends round and she and her boyfriend, Alastair, decided to go and see a film at the local cinema.

They started arriving around 7.30pm. Initially it was the familiar faces of my classmates with a few of their not-so-familiar friends on tow. The procession of people coming up my close stairs to our top flat gathered pace. Groups of people I'd never seen before started arriving, carry-outs of alcohol in hand. I was too young and naïve to deny them entry. Besides hadn't I blagged my way into strangers' parties myself on a few occasions? The living room was filling up, the youngsters encamped around on the floor, passing bottles and cans to each other. One swaggering, long-haired lad strolled into the living room. He tried to stifle a laugh as he tugged the ring-pull of his can of lager, showering my parents recently applied wallpaper in an alcoholic spray. A classmate tugged at my arm to tell me that in our dining room some people had opened the window and were entertaining themselves by throwing their empty beer cans at passers-by in the street, some fifty feet below. I walked frantically from room to room, each one increasingly packed with young people determined to have a good time. With the amount of alcohol being consumed bladders were quickly filling and a queue was forming outside the bathroom. I was later told that some inebriated lad in a fit of bravado had climbed up the outside drainpipe to try to gain access to the loo. Another desperado forced and broke the lock on the bathroom door only to find some drunken girl washing her hair over the bath. The mayhem was mounting. A couple of lads decided to explore our hall cupboard and pulled out my dad's golf clubs. It was when one them started to practise his golf swing on the hall carpet that a friend from school, Stuart, took me aside and advised me to phone the police. Overwhelmed and seriously out my depth, I dialled 999.

Mercifully the policeman was not long in coming. The sight of his uniform had the desired effect on the party animals and they obediently filed out of the flat. Across the landing from my front door lived an older couple. Their door was cautiously open and they peered out, watching the mass exodus. I will never forget the fear written all over the old man's face as he stood at his doorway, a poker gripped tightly and held aloft like a sword in case any of these young hoodlums should try to cross his threshold.

Fortunately, the flat was more or less empty by the time Fiona and Alastair returned from the local cinema but I still hadn't managed to extricate a couple who were having a romp in my bed. Alastair was not pleased. 'Get them out of there!' he roared. I got them to leave and, totally humiliated and ashamed, began the tidying-up operation.

When my parents returned the next day, I was surprised how easy-going they were about the whole affair. Thankfully a weekend of quiet meditation at their church retreat had rendered them full of Christian forgiveness. They could see that I wouldn't be attempting to have any more parties in the near future. Their gullible and naïve youngest son had hopefully learned a lesson.

———✦———

# 3 First Rung of the Ladder

*'It's very difficult for me to dislike an artist. No matter what he's creating, the fact that he's experiencing the joy of creation makes me feel that we're in a brotherhood of some kind… we're in it together.'*

*Chick Corea*

"Do something Colin!' Douglas Bryce, a boy from my school is looking up from the front of the audience, exasperated by my inept stage presentation. 'For God's sake, Colin, move!' Holding my flute nervously between my two hands I realise I have never considered what I might do on stage in the gaps when I'm not actually playing. These gaps are now feeling like an eternity and I'm standing stock still and feeling painfully unsure what to do with myself. I glance sideways at our singer, Jacky. He bears a striking resemblance to his hero; Robert Plant and he is doing his best to deliver all the rock singer trademarks of the day. With one hand he is punishing his right hip with a tambourine whilst the other holds the mic in an impassioned grip, his red, shoulder-length hair tumbling wildly over his anguished face as he hollers.

But now Jacky ramps it up further. It is now his left hand that is getting rhythmically punished by the tambourine as he brings a screaming chorus to a new level of frenzy. Following Jacky's lead, I take hold of the mic stand and start to shake my head, hoping my head-banging will demonstrate to the audience just how much I'm 'into the music'. Of course, every cell within me knows I am totally faking it.

In the dressing room afterwards Jacky is ecstatic, measuring the success of our performance by the blood now seeping from a wound in his tambourine-pulverised hand.

So ends the first and only gig of the band 'Parasite'. This took place at the Clarkston Halls in Glasgow's suburban south side. For weeks we had practiced up our repertoire, covering tunes by bands of the day; Cream, Jethro Tull, Family, East of Eden, each of us holding in our imaginations the youthful dream of fame and success.

Gavin played bass guitar in the short-lived Parasite and it was he, some months later, who found an opportunity to resurrect that youthful dream. The music shops in town, Cuthbertsons and Biggars had notice boards where local musicians could post messages. He had seen an advert, along the lines of:

'Guitarist and drummer seek bass player to form progressive rock band. Gigs at the ready. No time wasters.'

Gavin had given them a call and the guitarist, Jim, had said he'd be interested to audition a flute player as well.

A few days later Gavin and I took the bus into town and then the train from Queen Street Station to travel to Jim's house in Craigendoran on the outskirts of Helensburgh, a half-hour journey on the north side of the Clyde. Jim had given us instructions.

'Get off at Craigendoran, walk round the corner to Marmion Avenue. We're number 28, the one with the big hedge.'

Sure enough we found a distinctive, well-developed privet hedge obscuring the front of Jim's semi-detached bungalow. However, Gavin and I were both somewhat taken aback when the door opened. Standing in the hallway was the hairiest man we'd so far seen in those long-haired times. Just as the privet hedge masked the front of Jim's house so too did Jim's hair mask his face. It was an explosion of frizz, long to the shoulders but with an equally long fringe that made it difficult to see more than one of Jim's eyes at a time. The mouth under the fringe offered us a soft greeting and invited us in.

We squeezed into Jim's tiny back bedroom and heaved off our ex-army greatcoats. Jim sat on his bed and brought his semi-acoustic guitar onto his lap.

Jim Yule was a year or so older than us and had left school the previous summer. He had evolved a lifestyle that we could only dream of. Whilst we were caught up in the tedium of preparing for our Scottish Higher exams Jim slept in until midday, later even, then practised his guitar, dreaming up songs through the afternoon, evening and into the wee small hours. His guitar sat comfortably on him, like an extra limb. He played us some of his songs. His fingers danced over chord progressions we'd never encountered before. Then he played us a Stevie Wonder song, something he'd recently worked out, singing in a soft understated manner. Gavin and I couldn't believe our luck. Jim, with his brilliant musicianship and crazy hair surely was the ticket to our teenage dream of playing in a creative, interesting band. Soon he was showing Gavin the bass lines to his songs and coming up with ideas for what I could play on the flute. We seemed to have passed the audition as Jim suggested we could meet up next week with his mate, Woody, the drummer, and start building up a set. Gavin and I sat on the train as it rumbled back to Glasgow, the grey cloud of exam preparation now happily pierced through with the sunshine of new musical possibilities.

So began a weekly meeting in Woody's dad's sauna, a large wooden building on the edge of Craigendoran. Inside there was a pool and we set ourselves up to rehearse in between the relaxation beds. Woody turned out to be an affable Australian. Although we were learning Jim's material, we also practised up one of Woody's songs, a ballad named 'Grey Autumn' which he impressively sang whilst playing the drums. We learned a quirky array of songs honed from Jim's magpie musical interests, jazzy instrumentals to folk-tinged songs. Jim had a highly developed sense of the ridiculous and couldn't resist inserting silly tunes like the Teddy Bears' Picnic or the theme from Andrew Lloyd Webber's 'Jesus Christ Superstar' in between our more serious numbers. From an entertainment point of view this strategy later saved us on a few occasions when, for instance, we were playing in a working men's club and our self-penned repertoire was going down like a lead balloon with our very traditional audience.

It was after a few weeks that Jim had a suggestion for me. He liked the flute in the band but could I play saxophone as well? I warmed to the idea and at my next lesson with Solly I asked my teacher's advice. By lucky coincidence Solly's brother, Lazarus, had an alto saxophone, unused, lying in its case under his bed. Lazzy had developed asthma and was no longer able to play and was willing to sell me his old instrument for £60. I thus came into possession of a lovely 1931 Selmer 'Cigar-cutter' alto saxophone. It took me a few years to recognise how lucky I was to obtain such a classic instrument, Selmer saxophones being the Rolls-Royces of the sax world. It is the only alto saxophone I've ever owned and has been a constant companion through the past fifty years of playing.

Without any quibble from the rest of us Jim decided on a name for the band, 'UP'. Short and snappy, it had positive and cheerful overtones. Jim even came up with a poster, the letters UP in a trippy grid of purple and pink wavy lines in the pop-art style of Bridget Riley. Soon we had a manager, a local lad, Gordon. He was more old-school traditional than we scruffy musicians and his smart-suited look would surely open doors to future gigs. We also acquired a roadie. This was Mac, who seemed at ease with servicing leads, amplifiers and sourcing PA systems. Most importantly he had passed his driving licence and could hire us a van to get to gigs.

Meanwhile at school, there had been a small revolution based on the issue of hair length. The desire for boys to be allowed to let their hair grow long reached a point where a 'School Action Group' was formed. This was essentially a platform to assert pupils' rights. The ringleaders made a plan.

Every morning there was an assembly of all pupils in our main hall where all the classes would line up in rows facing the stage from where our headmaster, in front of the seated, black-gowned staff would make announcements. After the 'head's' announcements and the customary hymn it was the job of Mr Begg, the gym teacher to direct the organised filing out of the classes from the hall. The word got round to the whole school that when Mr. Begg started this routine that all pupils would refuse to leave. Suddenly Mr Begg was confronted by six hundred boys stamping their feet. When the foot stamping died down the bemused Mr Begg was heckled by some of the older boys demanding the right to let our hair grow long. He was obviously taken aback by this demonstration of strong feeling but surprisingly seemed to adopt a conciliatory attitude as he responded to the hecklers. Something had shifted and the School Action Group won the day.

There was another pressing personal issue still haunting me; my secret life in my dad's choir. My voice had broken and I had gone along with my father's suggestion that I sing alto for a period whilst my voice transitioned to bass. At least as an alto I no longer had to wear a frilly ruff like the choirboys but I was tormented by the possibility that my cool bandmates might find out. It all came to a head one weekend.

'Up' had been invited to play at the 21st party of a friend of Mac's. The party took place in Thornton Hall, a rather select area in the countryside to the south of Glasgow boasting more than its fair share of grand houses. At the end of the evening, I found myself entangled with the birthday boy's younger sister, Janie. It had been increasingly apparent that Janie was interested in getting me into her bed. This possibility, the Holy Grail for most young lads of a certain age and something I'd no doubt longed for over the past few years suddenly became a daunting prospect. Her bedroom was an enormous open-plan affair. Next to the large double bed there was an apparatus quite new to me; a bidet. Jane patiently explained its purpose as she climbed into bed and invited me to join her. Bypassing the bidet opportunity and crippled with shyness I decided to leave on my shirt and gingerly climbed onto the bed. She laughed good-naturedly, exclaiming 'you've still got your clothes on!' I didn't try to justify my behaviour, nor did I remove my shirt. I think Janey quickly realised this was going nowhere. Instead of getting serious we chatted, giggled and had a tentative cuddle before falling asleep.

The next morning was Sunday. I should be going church to sing in the choir. It was going to be very tricky to explain to my host where I was going. So, it was then, perhaps triggered by the small but significant rite of passage the previous night that I made the big decision. I had left the choir. When I returned home later that day my father, much to my surprise, accepted my decision without a flicker of questioning. Ten years of church services and choir practices had come to an end. It was decades later before I realised that those ten years had given me a musicianship that no university course or stint in a band could possibly have offered me.

The summer of 1971 was the year of the one-off free festival at Peaton Hill, somewhat incongruously sited on a disused military base above the Gareloch where the Trident Nuclear submarines are docked at Faslane. This festival was the brainchild of Davy Roy, son of the one-time local provost of Kilcreggan. Davy felt that a festival on the remote Kilcreggan peninsula would be just the thing to liven things up a bit. Davy was mates with Woody and Jim, so UP were given a booking to play. Other bands from Glasgow were invited including Brian Young's 'Northwind'. Brian was later on to establish Ca-va Studios, one of Glasgow most celebrated recording studios throughout the 70s and 80s.

Davy, without having passed his driving test, borrowed his dad's car to bring all the equipment, generator and PA system up to the site. A stage for the performers was hastily erected and a small village of tents had begun to mushroom around it. At the tender age of sixteen this was my first experience of festival life, where a whole bunch of young people, often of alternative persuasions, get together to express their notions of counter-culture, the most obvious examples of this being the imbibing of alcohol alongside mind-altering substances, and performances by bands doing their own new, radical music. I was, at that age, too wary of experimenting with drugs, having hardly as yet gotten used to the bitter taste of beer, but I could hardly avoid becoming aware of people at the festival behaving in, what could be called, 'liberated' ways. There were, of course, 'stoner' grins a-plenty with all the joints being passed around. Some people had 'dropped' tabs of acid and were gleefully tripping, finding fascination in the smallest detail of their surroundings.

When Up took the stage, I can remember feeling flattered that the clarinettist/saxophonist, Dick Lee, who later went on to make a successful career in swing music in Edinburgh, stood for a while at the front the stage, resplendent in a pink cape, apparently approving of what he was hearing. After our set I got chatting with him. It turned out he was doing a music degree at Glasgow University, a route I was beginning to consider for myself. He invited me back to his tent. The tent was full of recumbent humanity in various states of consciousness. In the gloom we picked our way over the bodies to the back of the tent where Dick found his alto saxophone. For some reason he chose to play some corny TV theme tune but the beautiful tone he produced still blew me away. I was transported back to the world of Paul Desmond, the celebrated sax player and composer of 'Take Five', whose sound my brother, Graeme had encouraged me to emulate.

The gigs for 'Up' started coming. Initially we played safe with pub venues which were known to put on bands. We seemed to get away with it. We were enthusiastic to reach out to new audiences and began to do university union gigs in Glasgow and Edinburgh, supporting the likes of the Irish guitar legend, Rory Gallacher at Strathclyde University. However, it gradually became apparent that our manager, Gordon, was happy to book the band in anywhere where we could get a fee. This took our essentially home-grown, prog-rock music into some incongruous places.

One such venue was the Clydebank 'Bankies' club, the social club for the football team, Clydebank. The Saturday night audience, used to a diet of chart songs and classic pop songs from the Elvis and Roy Orbison era tolerated only about three or four of our self-penned offerings before we had a deputation at the front of the stage.

'Can ye's no gie us some tunes we know? It's all married couples here.'

This wasn't so much a request, more of an order. We were ruining their precious evening out. One hardman eyeballed us intently, clearly not impressed with this bunch of privileged posh boys who couldn't even play a recognisable tune. Jim quickly launched into a song current at the time, 'Part of the Union' by the Strawbs which he hoped might pacify them. To some extent it worked and a few couples shuffled tentatively onto the dance floor. Unfortunately, we quickly exhausted our small fund of songs that might win them over. Menacing stares of disapproval were coming in our direction. Even the 'Teddy Bear's Picnic' somehow didn't float their boat.

We decided to take a break. It was at this point Gordon confided in us that there had actually been a murder outside the front door of the club on the previous week. Naturally our minds rushed to the grim conclusion that the unfortunate victim must have been a musician who had been dispatched for playing the wrong tunes. It became increasingly apparent that this was not an audience to piss off. Gordon advised us not to use the toilet in case someone had a 'go' at us. We made a quick decision; holding onto our full bladders, we quickly packed our gear and fled, leaving the Bankies club in the capable hands of the resident DJ.

By the time we were playing the Bankies' Club Gavin had long left school and gone to Glasgow University to study languages. I found myself in Sixth Form with a newly-formed resolution to make a life as a musician. The obvious path would be to go onto university to do a music degree.

This would necessitate doing my music 'higher' exam in one year. Since you could more or less design your own timetable in sixth form, I assigned myself about 25 periods of music, most of them self-study in order to get through the syllabus. Piano skills were also needed if I were to go on to University so back, I went to piano lessons with a sweet old lady round the corner from our home at Tantallon Road.

This was Gladys Henderson, who tutored me up to Grade Six level.

Kenny went off to study at St Andrew's University. One Easter, he contacted me with a proposition that a few of us go to the Isle of May. This would be our second trip there and I was already a convert to the island's magic spell. Two girlfriends of Kenny's from St Andrews would be coming along with Gavin, myself and Kenny's mate from Bearsden, Iain Fergus.

Coming from Glasgow to the Isle of May at Eastertime was nothing short of a change of worlds. The May is a kingdom of birds at this time of year with many species of seabird coming to breed on the island's steep cliffs. While the birds made their nests in every nook and cranny of the rocks and cliff faces, we humans were accommodated in the Low Light, the old lighthouse, a building maintained by the RSPB. Kenny, as a RSPB member, was allowed to reserve the accommodation for the week on the proviso that he did some bird counting. The rest of us were just there for the ride. Not that we didn't help, of course. Accompanying Kenny on his rounds of the island was interesting with the occasional unusual birds stopping off at the May on their flight across the North Sea from Scandinavia. We spent many a lazy hour on our bellies peering over the cliff edges and watching the comings and goings of kittiwakes, razorbills, shags and fulmars. A walk through the massive herring gull colony at the west of the island was a hair-raising experience with thousands of gulls objecting to our presence with raucous calls and occasional dive-bombing. On one occasion Kenny took us out after dark to ring puffins who had returned back to their burrows after a day at sea. We watched as Kenny plunged his arm into a burrow and pulled out an angry puffin. By the light from our torches, he managed to hold the struggling creature firmly enough to get a ring clipped onto one of its legs before depositing it back in its burrow.

After a day exploring the island, we would cook a communal meal and settle into the Low Light for the evening. A log of the day's activities was kept which we wrote up with a view to entertaining future visitors to the Low Light. We had a couple of guitars with us, whistles, jew's harps, my flute and saxophone and we would play some tunes, some of our old String Band favourites, songs from HMS Donovan amongst others. Iain and Kenny had been given the go-ahead to produce a multi-media show at the Cottage Theatre in Cumbernauld and were busy discussing possibilities and writing songs for the production. We made basic recordings on an audiocassette machine alongside a song that Gavin had written and some jigs and reels I was learning on the flute.

I had read somewhere in a book the story of a fiddler up in the north of Scotland who could charm the local seal population with his music, the sound of which enticed the seals out of the water to rest a while on the rocks as he played. I decided to give this a try and took my saxophone down to a rocky outcrop overlooking the sea. The head of a seal did surface, the seal gazing wonderingly at me for a few moments. He or she was not impressed and made no attempt to come any closer or clamber up a convenient rock to listen. I now imagine that if it were possible for seals to stay afloat whilst keeping their flippers over their earholes, that's what it would have done. It did the next best thing and disappeared under the waves.

We had a blissful week of entertaining company in a beautiful environment and were all sad to be leaving the following Saturday. The weather, however had different plans. On Saturday morning when the fishing boat should have been coming to fetch us back to Anstruther the wind picked up.

We looked out at the choppy waves and realised that it would have been too risky for the skipper to venture out today. Pleased to have another night on the island we managed to find enough food in our supplies to give ourselves a meal. The next day the wind had gone from bad to worse and it was blowing a gale. The full realisation of our predicament began to dawn on us. We were marooned on an island with our food supply almost used up. How long would this go on?

Fortunately, we were not alone on the island. The main lighthouse was still manned at this time and there were three lighthouse keepers. These men we had already befriended in the previous week. There was David, a small Orkadian man with an accent so impenetrable he may as well have been speaking another language. The other two men would also pop into the Low Light for a chat, no doubt glad of the change of company. One of them would take a seat and begin to fill his pipe. Kenny, who was also cultivating a pipe-smoking habit, would join him, the two of them filling the room with the aroma of tobacco.

As the second week progressed the storm showed no sign of abating. The wind was so strong you could lean at forty-five degrees into it and not fall over. The lighthouse keepers took pity on us and came to our aid. There was a healthy population of rabbits on the island and one day the keepers appeared at our door with a large dish of rabbit pie.

This we gratefully devoured. Another time they invited us up to the main lighthouse and gave us a meal there from their rations. Most of the time, however we had to get by with foraging. Fortunately, it was egg-laying season and in the nests on the cliffs and rocks there was a plentiful supply. Mostly the seabirds made their nests on the inaccessible cliff faces but we managed to find some shags' nests lower down on some rocks which could be reached with a bit of scrambling. We ate quite a few eggs that week and tried our luck with shellfish. I remember attempting to eat limpets which, in our ignorance, we had boiled for an hour. The over-cooking turned their flesh to the texture of indigestible, chewy rubber.

Wednesday came, then Thursday. Still the winds blew strong. The lighthouse keepers began to talk of getting us off the island by helicopter. When they contacted the air-sea rescue people they were told that the operation to fly out a helicopter to us would be too costly. Besides, they insisted, the weather would be better by the weekend.

Whilst we were no doubt very much enjoying the whole romance of being stranded on an island, Gavin and I had another pressing need to be getting back home. 'Up' had, a few weeks previously, entered a national band competition organised by Melody Maker magazine and had managed to get through the first two heats. The semi-final was happening that coming weekend, and with the final being staged in London it was potentially an important opportunity for us. Jim and Woody were understandably feeling worried we wouldn't get back in time.

Saturday came and to our relief the storm had finally dropped. Looking out over the sea towards the Fife coast the sea was once again calm. Later that morning we packed our rucksacks, said our goodbyes to the Low Light and made our way down to the landing stage. One of the lighthouse keepers was there to greet us with a message from the skipper of the fishing boat. Apparently, in spite of the improved weather he couldn't come to fetch us until the next day. East Fife, his favourite football team were playing an important fixture that afternoon, an event much more significant than rescuing a bunch of marooned teenagers and one he just wasn't prepared to miss.

# 4 Leaving Home

*'To some extent I happily don't know what I'm doing. I believe it's an artist's responsibility to trust that.'*

*David Byrne*

The music department of Glasgow University is housed at 14 University Gardens in a terrace just off University Avenue. I had become acquainted with the building having been invited in my sixth year of school to join a wind quintet from Shawlands Academy which happened to rehearse there on Friday nights. We would get a bus over to the West End from Shawlands and once there play through a variety of music, mainly as I recall, by twentieth century composers. It was a rich experience, getting up close to the sounds of bassoon, French horn, clarinet and oboe. The sonic world of the quintet helped me become more aware of the visual effect of music, how the imagination of the composer could, through the combination of harmony, rhythm and melody mysteriously evoke atmospheres, even a narrative, as you played.

I was therefore familiar with the music department's Edwardian elegance when I arrived in September 1973. I was pleased at last to have left school and to be moving forward in life. There were perhaps a dozen students in my year, including my mate from Hutchie, Robin, who had done his Higher music alongside me. There were some seriously good musicians amongst both staff and students in the department, some with streaks of genius. Whilst some students were destined to become run-of-the-mill music teachers, others had more flamboyant ambitions, perhaps to be composers or arrangers.

The professors at the music department encouraged the development of certain skills deemed to be key if one wanted to be a professional musician. Looking back, some of those skill-sets seem very specialist and arcane. One module was in figured bass, a skill associated with the baroque period where the keyboardist improvises his or her part according to the numbers written above the bass line. This I could relate to, as it seemed similar to the way a jazz musician would fill out the sequence of chords using a chart of symbols. Another module where we had to learn to harmonise in the manner of a chorale by J.S. Bach could prove useful in some future circumstances. However, reading at sight motets by the 16th century composer Palestrinas, with five simultaneous contrapuntal parts, each written in the alto or tenor clef; - that, for me was a tough call and not a skill I could ever see myself wanting to develop.

One day there was a buzz of anticipation in the department. Something called a synthesiser was being delivered. I watched, astonished, as the delivery men struggled to negotiate an enormous rectangular box through the front door and up the stairs. The new synthesiser was settled into a room on the first floor and we students were encouraged to get interested in it. Synthesisers and electronic music was touted to be an important new development and the music department prided themselves in obtaining such an up-to-date piece of kit. There was even a rumour that the synthesiser had come from the BBC radiophonic workshop which has spawned various scores, most famous being the original theme tune from the BBC TV series, Dr Who.  When I came to explore the synthesiser, I found the process of making music with it very laborious, involving complex 'patching in' of leads on a matrix board to produce different sustained tones. It sat in the room like a giant wardrobe with its indecipherable array on inputs and knobs. It's amazing to think there is more processing power in a modern smart phone than there was in the entire bulk of that enormous synthesiser.

Back in the seventies students had the luxury of receiving a grant to cover lodgings and food. There were no tuition fees payable. Compared with present-day students we definitely had it easier from a financial point of view. The music student undergraduates were also given a grant towards practical lessons on their chosen instrument. How lucky were we? It was expected that I'd put my money towards instrumental lessons. However, it didn't quite work out that way.

In the summer before I enrolled at university, I decided I should raise my game and take some lessons from a top flautist. My old teacher, Solly Banks was a great guy and had taught me a lot but was more of a multi-instrumentalist rather than a specialist flautist. I went to see Paul Kingsley, who was principle flautist with the Scottish National Orchestra. He gave me a couple of lessons before he confided in me that my progress on the flute was being hampered by the fact that I was carrying a lot of tension in myself. Apparently, my fingers were gripping the flute too tightly and my shoulders were hunching. He highly recommended that I take some lessons in something called the Alexander Technique. "Take a few lessons", he said as he handed me a business card, "Then come back and see me". I was a bit bemused, downcast even by this suggestion, and it wasn't without some reluctance that I called the number on the card.

My Alexander Technique teacher turned out to be a middle-aged but surprisingly youthful Danish man by the name of Aksel. In his teaching room there was a simple dining-style chair and a large flat couch upon which to lie. Once I was seated, he placed his hands gently around my neck and invited me to stand up out of the chair. His hands somehow re-organised my movement pattern. This process he repeated several times, all the time offering encouraging suggestions in his sing-song Danish accent, 'not to try too hard. Use less effort. Don't push with your legs,' and 'allow me to take you up out of the chair'. I hadn't much clue as to what was going on intellectually. All I know is that when I left the session I felt somehow altered, lighter and free in myself. I was to attend these sessions initially three times a week for three weeks, thereafter moving down to twice a week. Fortunately, I had just received my grant from the music department for practical music lessons and decided that I'd use the money instead to cover the Alexander sessions.

I became so fascinated with the possibilities of Alexander Technique that I continued to take lessons throughout the three years of my degree course. I began to realise that with all the instruments I had been playing over the previous ten years I had been unconsciously generating distortions and tensions in myself, hunching over guitars and pianos, twisting myself to play the flute. The lessons were consciousness-raising and I could feel a new inner confidence emerging within myself as I began to shed some of my teenage worries. The staff at the department never questioned how I was spending my grant. As far as I was concerned the lessons were helping me to play better with less unnecessary effort, so that was money well spent. I did hear sometime later however, that Paul Kingsley was disappointed that I never went to have more flute lessons with him.

The Alexander Technique chimed with the consciousness-raising climate of the times. Someone, perhaps Jim or Kenny, had encouraged me to read Lobsang Rampa's book, 'The Third Eye', which explored all things mystical including the author undergoing trepanation, having his head drilled into to open up his 'third eye', thus enabling him to see auras and to read peoples' minds. The book was later denounced as a hoax, having been written by the son of a plumber named Cyril Hoskin, who claimed that after falling out of an apple tree his body had been inhabited by the spirit of a Tibetan monk. Hoax or not, this book fired my imagination with the possibilities of changed consciousness. My Alexander teachers encouraged me to read 'Island', Aldous Huxley's Utopian vision of humanity, where Huxley outlined radical ways for young people to enter adulthood, through spending time away from their birth parents and undergoing a ceremony involving the ingesting of mind-altering mushrooms. Not that my AT teachers were condoning the use of drugs. They were just open-minded people, which, given their age, was refreshing to a young person like myself. A pivotal moment for me was one time observing Aksel getting out of his car and walking up the steps into his flat. I remember feeling surprised that someone in his fifties could move with such grace and lightness of being. It was a mystery how he could be like that, the secret of which I wanted to understand.

Shortly after I started my university course my grandmother, Granny Alice, moved out of her flat into a geriatric ward. It became apparent that she was unlikely to be able to live independently again on account of her severe dementia. My parents suggested that I could occupy her flat, thus keeping the house safe and providing me with free accommodation.

Her flat at number 14 Wilton Drive was something of a museum. The kitchen still had the original cooking range that would have been installed when the flats were built in the late nineteenth century. My father had moved there with his family around the end of the First World War. Nothing much had changed inside the flat since those days. The range was still heated by coal and to heat water I had to suspend a kettle from a metal arm and swivel it around over the flames.

In the parlour, or living room, there was a fine old upright piano, one that my father and aunt would have endlessly practised on in the days before their marriages. An aspidistra, an essential adornment in an Edwardian parlour, sat neglected in a large pot by the bay window. There was also an ancient sofa which converted, with some metallic grinding and groaning, into a rather lumpy double bed.

Here I had my first taste of independent living. My other Alexander teacher, Jeanne, wife of Aksel, helped with my conversion to vegetarianism and gave me some good advice regarding my first forays into cooking. White sugar was evil and to be avoided at all cost if one wanted to avoid an early death. Wholemeal flour and rice with fresh vegetables formed the basis of many of my early cooking experiments. I discovered I quite liked cooking. I remember one of my specialities was to roast almonds carefully over the range and enjoy them with mashed potato and cabbage.

Kenny and I would visit Iain, our fellow Isle of May strandee in Bearsden. Iain was a longhair and budding songwriter who had come through the Incredible String Band thing. A few of us typically would go for walks from Iain's house out to Mugdock Castle, sometimes with instruments, hang out in the old ruins and practise songs. Iain was just experimenting initially but over time his confidence grew and his songs became stronger. There was one I liked, 'Open the Door to Mystery', very much in a Robin Williamson mould and another, 'Building a Motorway', a protest song about the desecration of the landscape with the building of a new expressway from Glasgow out to Loch Lomond. I remember after one of our Mugdock afternoon gatherings, sitting in someone's house around a primitive machine to record a couple of his songs. The intention was to send the songs off to John Peel. We added in a silly version of The Archers theme tune. This ironic, tongue-in-cheek offering, Iain felt, was right up John's street. He wouldn't be able to resist playing it. As far as I know John Peel's very broad taste in innovative music never went so far as to include our humble, badly-recorded offerings and the audio cassette no doubt lay in his studio amongst all the other dodgy recordings from young musicians around the UK, in a box marked 'UNWORTHY'.

Undaunted by John Peel's shameful lack of interest, Iain started to pick up gigs and invited me along to play flute. I developed a way of weaving lines in between his vocal phrases which I hoped added something to the songs.

One gig with Iain I remember was in Cumbernauld Theatre. They must have been a very enterprising and forward-thinking organisation to take the risk of booking us 'unknowns'. Ian had come up with a name for the band, the very splendid 'New Celeste'. I remember going to the gig on the bus, awkwardly carrying instruments and bits of kit, thinking, 'there is something wrong here. Where are the roadies and the van?' Actually, the gig went down well. In spite of travelling to the gig on the bus we came across as professional, and our endearing, callow youthfulness secured 'New Celeste' return bookings.

It was on a visit to Ian's that I again met up with Ronnie whom I'd met a few years before round at Kenny's house when we were both 15. Ronnie Goodman was a drummer in a prog-rock band and looked the part with his long hair tumbling around his shoulders. He had been living down in London for three years leading the rock and roll lifestyle. Now, sitting in Iain's living room he caught my attention. He had his guitar with him, painted a peacock blue, upon which he showed me a complex chord sequence he had invented, all the time looking at me intensely to gauge my reaction. I recalled the crass joke that was going around at the time: 'What's the definition of a drummer? Someone who hangs around with musicians'. But here was a drummer who had developed quite a technique on the guitar. Ronnie was someone with yearning musical ambitions and we became good friends. He had an expansive interest in music, beyond the prog-rock that he was currently playing.

Round at his house one day he took me aback slightly by confiding that his favourite music was Brazilian. I had already narrow-mindedly closed the door on Brazilian music, deciding it had an airport-lounge, predictable smoothness that belonged to a previous generation. Ronnie put an album on the turntable which turned my fixed idea completely around. This was 'Butterfly Dreams' by Airto Moreira and Flora Purim. This music was a revelation to me, a delicious serving up of exotic sounds played by jazz musicians at the top of their game. There were great tunes in there with beautiful chord progressions but all stretched out into a dreamy, other-worldly way, the musicians able to float freely and creatively over the changes. Technically it was beyond me back then but I stored that musical landscape inside me somewhere and was able, to some extent, to enjoy its influence in years to come when shaping my own musical ideas.

It was Jim Yule who came up with the idea for a busking holiday. It was the summer before I began university and with the yawning space between leaving school and starting university it seemed a good idea. My brother, Brian, and his wife, Janet, were living in Tooting Bec, South London and were happy to accommodate us for a week. We couldn't afford the bus or train so hitching a ride was our only option. Besides, hitch-hiking seemed somehow in keeping with the spirit of a busking holiday.

We started our journey at Calder Park Zoo out beyond Glasgow's east end, hoping to pick up a lorry travelling south on the A 74. Looking at Jim standing at the side of the road with his crazy hair I began to have serious doubts as to whether anyone would stop for such a weird-looking person. We had several lifts on the way down to London and to my surprise it was Jim who had more success than me at getting people to stop. I guess he just looked more interesting. We spent a successful week travelling into central London from my brother's flat, sometimes busking in the subways at Marble Arch or Green Park where the acoustics were favourable and sometimes venturing into the closely packed streets of Soho. I played flute and Jim, guitar, expanding on our repertoire from the 'Up' tunes that we already knew well. We made a modest but worthwhile income. One diner even invited us into a restaurant. We serenaded him and his girlfriend over lunch for which he rewarded us handsomely.

The journey back north did not go so well. By the end of the first day, we had only managed to get to a village just a few miles north, in London's suburbs. We slept in the open under a tree on the village green. After an early start we picked up some lifts, one of which was in a maggot lorry. We had to sit in the back. There were no maggots, the driver having dropped his delivery earlier, but the smell was awful. No doubt the driver was chuckling away to himself in his cab, fully aware of the terrible whiff in the back of his lorry that the two young hippies had to endure. Things went from bad to worse. In a fit of misjudged desperation, we took another lorry which drove us over to the East of England. With various lifts we ended up in Dunbar in the Scottish borders, late at night and with the prospect of another night in the open. We wandered around the town, contemplating sleeping on the golf course before deciding that a bus shelter was a better option. We lay down in our sleeping bags on the concrete floor and managed to drift asleep. Several hours later we were surprised and somewhat embarrassed to wake up and find a queue of people standing around us, waiting for the morning bus. We clambered out of our bags and, ignoring their disdainful looks, made the quick decision to board the bus to Edinburgh. To get back home by spending some of our hard-earned busking money on the ticket seemed by that point, well worth it.

My first 'serious' girlfriend was a girl called Sheena. She was lovely. She invited me down to Arran later that same summer after Jim and I had returned from London. I was to camp while she stayed with her two aunts in a house in Sannox on the North east of the island. We had a good time, taking long walks, swimming off Sannox's deeply shelving beach or going out into the bay in a rowing boat.

The first few days I had my tent pitched in a small copse of trees next to a burn. Before drifting off to sleep I would hear what I thought were voices coming from the main road, which was not far off on the other side of the burn. I assumed they were the voices of people returning from the village pub. It was only later that I realised it was actually the river talking to me. In that drowsy state that one enters before falling asleep I had interpreted the ripplings and gurglings of the stream as human speech. It struck me that in more superstitious times someone would have assumed it was the fairies talking or even perhaps a pair of river goddesses having a gossip.

I moved away from the talkative river and set up camp on a level grassy area above the beach. Jim turned up and squeezed himself and his guitar into my tent.

Sheena and I decided we were up for an adventurous walk, something which Jim, with his thirty-fags-a-day habit was definitely not used to. The aunts gave the three of us a lift to Catacol in order to do the walk up a burn into the island's interior. It was quite a climb, taking us two or three hours. Jim was struggling and couldn't quite get why we would punish ourselves in such a way. Finally, above the tree-line we got to our destination, Loch Tanna. For the uninitiated the landscape up there is perhaps barren and monotone, the loch itself, a trifle bleak and lonesome with its black peaty shoreline. Jim declared it was 'Hell on Earth' and after a quick fag break couldn't wait to get back to civilization.

At the tent the next day Jim was once more on form and I can remember us sitting in the sunshine above the beach as he played me two John Lennon songs, 'It's Only Love' and 'Oh Yoko'. I've always admired how some musicians can, with their voice and a guitar, deliver that whole package of a song, the rhythmic drive of the strumming and the spontaneous inflections of the voice responding 'in the now.' Jim had that gift and these two songs have been etched in my mind ever since.

I can't quite recall when Mary seduced me. It certainly was some time in first year at university. She was, by my standards at the time, considerably older than me, she being 25 and me still a callow youth of 19. Most of my friends had started sexual relationships by then but for some reason I was slow to get round to this. Perhaps keeping my clothes on when in bed with young women didn't help matters. In my innocence I didn't realise at first that Mary was different from most other women. She wasn't really interested in romantic love. Just sex. Lots of it. Not that I was complaining. A young man of 19 has a good sex drive, which, of course, is probably what she saw in me.

It was all quite strange. Mary was sophisticated and somewhat theatrical, quite different from those of my own age-group. I never felt she was my girlfriend and I don't think she even expected that. She assured me she didn't have a boyfriend but as it turned out she had at least another two men in her life who were most put out that she had started hanging around with me. They were both upset and confused at what was going on, perhaps hoping that some love and affection was going on in their relationships with Mary. But no, looking back, it seems it was just physical pleasure she was after.

One time, around at my Granny's flat, there was an incident that still makes me feel mortified and sad in equal measure all these years later. It was mid-afternoon and Mary had once again come around for a decadent time with her young nineteen-year-old lover. Suddenly, from the bed we heard the sound of the front door opening. 'Coo-ee' came the voice at the door. It was my Auntie Effie, who, as she lived in the next street, had a key to the flat. ''Are you in, Colin?' her voice called out. Quick as a flash the naked Mary was out of the bed and hidden, giggling and shivering, in the cupboard whilst I hastily pulled on clothes.

I still feel terrible to this day that on the one time my sweet Auntie had come round to see how her nephew was getting on I was too flustered to even offer her a cup of tea.

I mumbled through a brief conversation, my body language transparently indicating some secret embarrassment and discomfort. She quietly excused herself and left.

# 5 From Up to a Mississippi Steamship

*'Sometimes I wish I could walk up to my music for the first time, as if I'd never heard it before. Being so inescapably a part of it, I'll never know what the listener gets, what the listener feels, and that's too bad.'*

*John Coltrane*

I'm sitting in an ancient stone-built 'black-house' a few miles East of Kirkwall, in Orkney. The walls, perhaps six to eight feet thick are unlined, the massive rocks put in place centuries ago by farmers determined to keep out the incessant Orkney wind. I'm relaxing with members of 'Up'. An American guitarist-songwriter by the name of J.J. Cale is on the turntable, bemoaning his dealings with the drug, cocaine.

To understand why 'Up' are in a black-house in Orkney we have to go back a few months.

In Glasgow, a band competition organised by Clydefest is taking place in an old cinema hall near the Eglinton Toll. After our performance we are called over to chat with the lead singer from one of the other bands. He has a proposition for us. Jim Wilkie is older than us, possibly mid-twenties, long-haired and bearded and with an air of someone who has been round the block a few times. He cuts to the chase; would we consider joining forces with his band, 'Dog Eat Dog'? He goes on to explain that, apart from his bass player, Charlie, his band is splitting up and he needs new musicians. His initial proposition makes us wary. After all, 'Up' is doing well as it is. We have just got through to the next round of the Clydefest competition, whereas Dog Eat Dog has not. Then, when Jim throws his trump card announcing that he could mount a major Scottish tour of the Highlands and Islands, our curiosity is aroused. Jim proposes that on the tour both bands would do a set and we'd split the profits. He goes on to explain that the remote communities up north will be grateful for new bands to show up and gigs should be well attended. Two weeks of touring Scotland, playing in exotic, far-flung places begins to appeal.

Jim is a mover and shaker. He has good connections throughout Scotland having previously worked at the Skye-based socialist-leaning newspaper, the West Highland Free Press. He promotes and organises tours for the successful mainstream folkies, The Corries. He also has ambitions as a singer-songwriter-performer, Dog Eat Dog having just completed ninety gigs in the previous hundred days. There are misgivings regarding the proposed tour, however. We need some time to make a decision. Since Jim would be bringing his own bass player, Charlie, Gavin feels he will be drawing the short straw; we three other 'Up' members get to play two sets and he will get to play only one. In time, however, the possibility of new experience and adventure wins Gavin over and we agree to go ahead with Jim's plan.

In the summer of 1974, we travel up Scotland's East Coast, playing gigs in various coastal towns like Tain and Wick on our way to Orkney where we stay a couple of days in the aforementioned black house. On the second leg of the tour we travel down Scotland's West side, taking in gigs on Lewis, Uist, Skye and Campbeltown. Mostly we manage to get a bed for the night but sometimes, after a performance in a village hall we have to sleep on the stage. I have a memory of Charlie the bass player, who has come on tour without a sleeping bag, laughing to himself as he stepped into the long plastic cover from one of the PA speakers to use as a form of bedding.

The assumption that audiences would be appreciative of new music turning up on their doorstep generally holds true. We feel we are offering a good package for the ticket price. 'Dog Eat Dog's set is very different from the jazz-tinged, prog-rock of 'Up', covering a very different style of music, rockier material by the likes of The Doors and the Allman Brothers. However, in Wick, in the far northern corner of Scotland, the formula of having two bands with musicians in common comes unstuck. 'Up' finish their set having gone down reasonably well with the audience. But when we take to the stage as 'Dog Eat Dog' we only manage one tune before there is a murmur of disapproval from the floor. Somebody heckles,

'It's the same band!'

Obviously, some people in the audience quite reasonably need convincing that a change of bass player and the addition of a singer constitutes a different band. We plough on, distancing ourselves as far as possible from the quirky, jazzy nuances of Up, quickly reinventing ourselves as the edgiest rock band ever to turn up in Caithness serving up as loud a version of 'LA Woman' as we possibly can in the hope of drowning out any discontent from the sceptical unbelievers in the audience.

Playing with 'Up' and 'Dog Eat Dog' was giving me a slice of musical education; holding arrangements in my head, listening and responding in the moment to other band members and occasionally to wing out on a 'solo'. The people in the music department in University Gardens, however, were presenting me with a whole different approach to the art of music making. The syllabus itself was very traditional with its exploration of musical development over the past five hundred years. However, staff and students did open my ears to things new.

Lectures on minimalist musicians like Steve Reich and Terry Riley's ground-breaking album 'A Rainbow in Curved Air' were interesting. A friend on the course, Alastair McNeill, introduced me to the music of John McGlaughlin and painstakingly taught me one of McGlaughlin's brain-stretching chord sequences on the piano. Another fellow student, Bob Stuckey, was a jazz musician who had played Ronnie Scott's London jazz club with the legendary South African saxophonist, Dudu Pukwana. He invited me to jam with him on flute whilst he laid down some nice sequences on his Wurlitzer electric piano. On another occasion Alastair invited a bunch of us to a session where we played Frank Zappa tunes. Alastair had scored it all out for us. Being reasonably competent readers, we made a passable attempt at Zappa's complex and quirky pentatonic creations.

It was all very diverse and stimulating and all these experiences were broadening my musical palette. However, the romance of playing in a band still remained my main focus.

Up have been invited to play the Kelvingrove Bandstand. This is another free festival, with a variety of bands playing throughout the afternoon and evening. I have a chance to hear Dick Lee playing. Dick has just graduated from the music department and is fronting a band, the splendidly named, 'Vladivostock'. They play the classic 'Take Five', Dick's luminous saxophone tones floating out into the auditorium, again recalling the mighty Paul Desmond.

A huge crowd of several hundred is filling the municipal amphitheatre. This is Glasgow's response to the rise of festival culture, a relatively new phenomenon sparked by events at Glastonbury, Bath and the Isle of Wight.

I notice a young woman going through the crowd, placing gum-backed, golden star-stickers on people's foreheads, perhaps to remind them of their 'inner elf' or maybe to awaken their 'third eye'. I observe her for a few moments as she goes about her consciousness-raising mission having, of course, no idea that six years later I will be married to her.

Another band takes the stage. The sun comes out from behind a cloud and the lead guitarist, with an appropriate American accent exhorts into the mic, 'c'mon everybody, let's hear it for the sun!' A unifying applause ripples through the crowd, shirts get removed and the spirit of Woodstock has arrived, for a while at least, in Presbyterian Scotland.

Up's quirky amalgam of jazz-tinged tunes with its odd sprinkling of novelty numbers which bizarrely includes the Benny Hill Theme tune, (originally called 'Yackety Sax' but now re-christened as 'Yackety Axe' by guitarist, Jim), goes down well with the crowd. This is Up's finest hour. As we sense the warm appreciation of the crowd we wonder if fame and recognition are just around the corner.

Gavin has noticed that there is a problem with our name. He has spotted an advertisement for a gig in the Melody Maker which lists another band by the name of UP. Apparently, Jeff Beck, the legendary guitarist, sometimes plays with them. They must be really good. This is alarming news. Gavin duly dispatches a letter to the Melody Maker, claiming that we've had the name longer than Jeff Beck's mates and listing some of the gigs we've done over the past while. It is very satisfying, a couple of months later, to see in the paper another gig advertised by the imposter band, now calling themselves UPP.

Several months later Up are booked to appear in an old cinema off the Maryhill Road. Again, several bands are playing, the event being something like an indoor version of the Kelvingrove Festival. We find our way to the communal dressing room. A couple of guys, their hair down to their waists and looking like fully paid-up members of the Hell's Angels have already ensconced themselves on the dressing room's only chairs. They are friendly enough. On the window ledge to my right the sun is illuminating what I assume to be three or four pints of lager. Somebody makes a comment on their ready supply of alcohol. In an accent, possibly Forfar or Airdie we are told it's best not to touch these. 'We couldna' be bothered goin' tae the lav', one announces with a wry smirk. These lads, aptly and provocatively named 'The Sleaze Band' take to the stage and deliver a set in keeping with their lifestyle, a hard-edged wall of sound, like they've revved up their Harley Davidsons and left the engines running.

After Up has done its set, I join Mary in the audience. This is the first time she has seen the band and I ask for her reaction. She mischievously ignores commenting on the music, preferring to admire the dexterity of my fingers on the saxophone's keys.

A duo takes the stage. These are two musicians whose lives I am soon to be entwined with, Stuart MacKillop and Alasdair Robertson. Today, they are the somewhat pretentiously named 'The Original Mystical Orchestra', no doubt a tongue-in-cheek reference to the Incredible String Band. Like Robin and Mike these two are multi-instrumentalists playing their own material. Later, we end up chatting backstage. Seemingly Stuart plays in another band, Joe Cool. 'We've got a great singer, Maggie Reilly' Stuart enthuses. He tells us he liked 'Up's music and begins to sound us out about the possibility of forming a new band with Maggie. From this brief encounter emerges a band that is to take over my life for the next three years.

Granny Alice, after several months confined to a bed in the geriatric ward finally slipped away in the summer of 1974. I'd lost my gypsy granny with her gentle manner and swarthy complexion, our granny who saw our futures in the pattern of tea leaves at the bottom of our cups on our Sunday afternoon visits. No longer did we have someone in our family, born all those years ago in Victoria's reign, who could tell us about the great Glasgow Exhibition of 1901, with its spectacular displays in Kelvingrove Park.

On a practical level my granny's passing left me homeless. In common with many people back then her flat had been rented from a 'factor' and had to be vacated. Fortunately, I'd befriended a group of folks, Simon, Morag and Sheila, who shared a flat in Gibson Street. As luck would have it, Sheila had recently decided to move out making it possible for me to take over her room. The rent was £3 per week, payable to the landlord who happened to be one of the waiters in the Indian restaurant below; the Koh-i-Noor. I moved myself and my inheritance from Granny Alice, her 1920's upright piano, into my new bedroom.

Simon and Morag were welcoming and friendly. Morag with her fair skin and long wavy red hair, half pre-Raphaelite model and half-Viking maiden, occupied a tiny room beyond the kitchen. Simon had the mixed fortune of having, as his bedroom, what would have been the lounge in a normal family household. Because it was large and spacious everybody tended to congregate there, a situation he mostly tolerated. Simon had ambitions to be a sound engineer but was often out of work and consequently, restless. His favourite utterance at the time was 'I'm bored'. He would fix his gaze on me and tell me this on an almost daily basis, his voiced tinged with pent-up frustration.

The flat itself was in a bad state. If you dropped a ball in a corner of Simon's room it would obediently roll down to the opposite corner, such was the degree of subsidence in the building. It was on the second floor on the end of the tenement block. It is no longer there. A few years after we moved out a crack appeared in the outside wall and the whole lot fell into the River Kelvin.

In our kitchenette there were a couple of sizeable rat holes. These would be regularly patrolled by Morag's handsome, snow-white tomcat, 'Strider'. Gibson Street at the time was known as 'Curry Valley' on account of its proliferation of curry houses. We were told that the basement of the 'Koh-i-Noor' below us was alive with rats. I came back to the flat one time to find Strider in our tiny kitchen, licking his lips, and exhibiting a large bulge in his stomach. Incredulously, I surveyed the floor and came to the realisation that all that was left of Strider's meal was the rat's tail and, shockingly, a pair of rat's eyes connected by some membranous tissue, staring into the void.

The new band has taken over Simon's room, the only room big enough in my flat to accommodate six musicians and their equipment. The long-suffering Simon has traded the use of his room as a rehearsal space with the promise that he will become the new band's roadie. Davy, of Peaton Hill fame, and who replaced Woody as Up's drummer, is sat behind his Premier drum-kit with its pink, mother-of-pearl, lacquer finish. With his long hair and moustache, he wouldn't be out of place in an old-time, Wild-West show. Stuart, short, with elfin features, has finished setting up his 73-key Fender Rhodes electric piano and is rehearsing through a sequence of chords for a song he has written. Gavin and I have finally achieved the long-haired look that we longed for as schoolboys, our hair reaching our shoulders but with our fringes respectably short, a pair of mediaeval page boys. Maggie has found a seat and is busy with some knitting needles. At her feet is Dill the dog, a mongrel pup that she and Stuart have adopted. We all momentarily pause to listen as Alan, blue eyed and handsome in a light shirt adjusts the settings on his amp. He purses his lips in concentration and out pours a stream of phrases from his Gibson 'Les Paul' guitar, the sound sustained and clean, reminiscent of Carlos Santana. A frisson of excitement passes through us all. Stuart suggests we run through one of his songs and hands out chord charts. Stuart, having worked with Maggie the previous two years knows how to hone a song to suit Maggie's voice. She and Stuart play it through to let us hear 'how it goes'. Maggie's voice floats above Stuart's chiming Rhodes chords, shades of Diana Ross' melting sweetness but occasionally displaying the edgy roughness of Janice Joplin.

The excitement is tangible and without needing to discuss it further we have all, within these few short moments, committed ourselves to each other. The potential of this combination of musicians fires up all our imaginations. We've all done our apprenticeships; Stuart and Maggie with Joe Cool; Davy, Gavin and myself in Up. Alan has been developing his sound playing with bands in Edinburgh. Gavin and Davy are a strong rhythm section, working well together. With not just one, but two trump cards in Maggie's voice and Alan's guitar, surely this band could go places.

Whilst I could supply colour and instrumental lines on sax and flute, maybe the occasional 'solo', Stuart encourages me to also contribute songs. I relish the opportunity. Who wouldn't?

Things start to gather momentum. Alan happily agrees to quit his civil engineering job and make the move to Glasgow. Within a couple of weeks, he has moved into the flat next door at no 4, Gibson Street. Davy persuades his old friend John Davies from Kilcreggan to come on board as our manager. The repetition and predictability of John's Day job as an optician is no match for the potential glamour of managing a band with interesting prospects. As for Simon he is, at last, no longer bored. He starts what eventually becomes a lifetime career in sound systems as our official roadie and sound engineer.

Soon after our formation we are approached by Stuart's friend, Alasdair Roberston, he of The Original Mystical Orchestra. Alasdair has recently finished a degree in English at Glasgow University and is keen to be a writer. He proposes that he could furnish Stuart and I with lyrics for songs. Very soon I have a bunch of Alasdair's lyrics on the music stand of my granny's piano and I'm making my first forays into song writing.

My music taste at this time was very wide and diverse. I was listening to albums by George Duke, Flora Purim and had recently discovered The Crusaders. These were great musicians, pushing forward the boundaries of music. They were not, however, bands that were known for producing chart material. The Average White Band became, in some ways, a model that we could perhaps follow, a Scottish band that were rising stars, with their first love of funk-driven, soul music taking them towards global success and fame. Steely Dan were also emerging at this time with great songs, painstakingly produced and played by the cream of America's session musicians; tuneful, commercially successful, yet seemingly without any compromise given to the pop music industry.

Maggie, Stuart and I were all blown away by the Joni Mitchell albums of this mid-seventies period. Her two albums, 'Court and Spark' and 'The Hissing of Summer Lawns' were high points in her career, her achingly beautiful songs coloured by the artistry of Tom Scott's horn arrangements, Joe Sample's tasteful Rhodes playing and

Larry Carlton's unique palette of haunting guitar phrases that swooped and dived around Joni's vocals. Alan became a Larry Carlton devotee, particularly loving his stunning solos with The Crusaders.

Talented musicians were putting up signposts all around us, each pointing us towards new musical directions. Chaka Khan had just released her first album 'From Rags to Rufus'. John McGlaughlin's Mahivishnu Orchestra made a huge impact on us, Davy becoming overnight an acolyte of their drummer, Billy Cobham.

There were so many great musicians around to influence us at this period. Our willingness to embrace all this outpouring could be seen as a good thing from an experimental and creative point of view. Ultimately, however, without a clear decision on which direction we were heading our potential for recognition and success would be under question. We were perhaps too busy enjoying playing music together and receiving positive feedback from our first gigs to see the bigger picture, each of us assuming that only a bright, glittering future for this band could possibly lie ahead.

# 6 Young Hopefuls

*'When the power of love overcomes the love of power the world will know peace.'*

*Bob Marley*

So many bands which I've been part of, and there have been many down the years, have struggled to find the right name for themselves. Several weeks have now gone by and our new band remains nameless. Perhaps this says something about the lack of clarity we have in terms of our musical direction and vision. Eventually Stuart's suggestion wins the day, 'Cado Belle'. The name of an old-time Mississippi steamboat is about as culturally removed from a bunch of young people in the West of Scotland as you could get.

Cado Belle spend most of 1975 working throughout Scotland from our Glasgow base, kept busy with gigs in a variety of venues; music pubs, colleges, universities, art centres and village halls. We clock up about 100 gigs that year. Many of the venues gave us return bookings; Tiffany's, an old dance hall in Edinburgh have us play there some sixteen times during the band's lifespan.

In the summer of '75, Jim Wilkie organises another Highlands and Islands tour for us and we travel to Islay to play in Port Ellen, the island's capital. So confident are we of impressing the local islanders, certain that they will feel lucky to have such a 'happening' band from the big city grace their village hall stage that we are booked to play here for two nights in a row. The first night the hall is crammed with people. We take to the stage to deliver our set, fully expecting to win immediate approval. The crowd wants to dance and it begins to become apparent that our tunes are not hitting the spot. We have mediocre applause after each song and some of the people seem to have drifted outside the hall to have a chat with their mates. The young woman who has liaised with Jim to have the band come and play is looking very uncomfortable. It becomes increasingly apparent that we are not producing the sounds she was expecting. She gets quite drunk and wanders a couple of times onto the stage insisting to Maggie that we play more chart material. We ignore her and finish our set without any compromise.

The second evening in Port Ellen we turn up to find we have an audience of just three or four people. Someone has deliberately organised a ceilidh in one of the other island villages and everyone has gone there. We give our tiny audience a short private performance after which we all head down to the local beach to drink a few beers with them and watch the waves.

Looking back at our 'snubbing' by the people of Islay I can admire the fact that there existed a strong traditional culture on the island at the time and that accordions and fiddles were preferable to this unknown band from

Glasgow. However, it did dent our pride a little which, of course, is always a good thing when you are getting too self-assured.

That same summer we travelled to Arran to play the halls in the three main villages on the island's eastside; Brodick, Lamlash and Whiting Bay. Because the summer population changes with the coming and going of holidaymakers, we could get away with doing this mini-tour three times over the season. No rival ceilidhs were organised on the other side of the island. The Arran venues had been part of the national band circuit for decades and well-known bands would sometimes show up. I could remember back in the late sixties, aged around thirteen, being on the ferry to Brodick with The Kinks on board. There was Ray Davies, writer of so many iconic songs, leaning on the boat's side-rail, staring pensively down into the foam created by the boat's wake. I wondered if he was getting inspiration for a song.

The Arran gigs are organised by Jimmy Moon and Jack Milroy, two fugitives from the big city who have sought the good life and settled themselves in Arran. Jack and Jimmy are into their music. Jack has a 'listening corner' in his cottage where he would sit and envelop himself in his vinyl collection. It was in this corner I first hear Ann Peebles singing her classic 'I can't stand the Rain'. Those opening Hammond organ lines still send shivers down my spine. When we are round at Jimmy's for a meal one evening, he gives us our first taste of some new music from Jamaica. On first hearing 'The Wailers' I have to admit I am confused. Underneath Bob Marley's strangely accented patois, nowadays accepted as mainstream pop, his music on first listening seems all wrong, the beats accenting a different part of the bar, loping along in a strangely disjointed way. It takes a few listens before I became a committed fan.

It is well known that Bob Marley's Rastafarian culture sees the smoking of marijuana as a religious sacrament. We didn't see marijuana in quite the same way but nevertheless most of us had by this time begun to indulge in the occasional joint. Smoking dope wasn't just a hedonistic escape. It came from a curiosity to experience something new, to perhaps gain new perspectives on things. I can remember that it did open new doors, the mundane things in my surroundings made fascinating, and sometimes a source of inspiration and wonder. The problem was remembering all these exciting thoughts and revelations once the dope had worn off.

Typically, at our home base in Glasgow, if Cado Belle was not playing a gig we would be rehearsing. After an afternoon rehearsal we would, in the evening, have a couple of pints at one of the local pubs, which at that time in accordance with Scottish drinking regulations closed at 10pm. Then we might head to Curry Valley for a meal in one of the restaurants there. After that, if we had any energy left, Davy's flat at Buckingham Terrace in Great Western Road was the place to go.

Davy lived there with his father, who seldom made an appearance, no doubt seeking refuge somewhere else, well away from the comings and goings of Davy's pals. We'd all pile into his living room and it wouldn't be long before Davy would put on an album by either Jimi Hendrix, Billy Cobham or perhaps the Mahivishnu Orchestra. We'd sit around on his well-worn sofas and somebody might roll a joint. All kinds of laddish silliness would then ensue. Davy would usually get the ball rolling, often with one of his favourite post-pub activities; fart lighting. I couldn't believe what I was seeing when I first saw Davy seated on his sofa lift up his legs to thrust forward his rear end and hold his cigarette lighter at the ready, his face contorted in deep concentration. A second later the lighter would ignite the methane and there would be a quick burst of coloured flame. Different colours could be produced. This would open up a discussion on what food had been eaten. Soon more arses were lifted and a kind of competition to produce the largest and most colourful flame would evolve. This activity, perhaps not being the most intellectual of pursuits would bring some members of the company to the decision that it was time to go home. If Davy felt you were not appreciating his idea of fun, he would be ready for you at his upstairs window with a saucepan of water ready to pour over you as you closed the door in the street below. To fall foul of this prank meant a soaked and miserable walk home and you only let Davy catch you out once.

There was one particularly memorable water fight. It started with a cupful of water being tipped over some one's head. Revenge had to be taken and before long we were all running around armed with cups full of water, hurling them at each other with mixed success. Davy decided to up the game a notch and grabbed a bucket. He managed to catch Gavin unawares and drench him. Gavin was speechless with rage and retreated into the bathroom where he found another plastic bucket. His clothes being completely wet he stripped down to his underpants. Intent on giving Davy the ultimate soaking, he kicked open the bathroom door, his filled bucket ready to hurl, shouting, 'Right, you bastard…' The expletive did not fully leave his lips. Standing directly opposite Gavin, having just climbed up the stairs was Davy's father and mother The looks on both Gavin's face and that of Davy's parents were priceless. It was a comedy classic.

Meanwhile, when we were not bonding over water fights and flatulence-ignition at Davy's flat, Cado Belle were putting the hours in. The songs were coming thick and fast. I think Stuart and I wanted to write something dance-orientated, something funky but more often our songs gravitated towards a mid-tempo groove. We booked ourselves into Brian Young's fledgling Ca-Va recording studios, at that time, still based at his home in Sanda Street. The demos sounded promising.

My girlfriend at this time was Claudia. She worked at the BBC for her radio producer boss, Stuart Conn. Claudia passed some of our demos to Stuart and he agreed to do a programme on us. To promote the programme the Radio Times ran a double page feature in their Scottish edition. I think it was my mum's proudest moment.

Later in the year, John began to reel out his managerial fishing rod over the pool of record companies based in London, our songs, hopefully, an attractive enough bait. Eventually we got a bite, not the biggest fish in the pond, a small but successful company called Anchor Records. Anchor was based in Wardour Street in central London and had had a major hit with one of their signings, a band called Ace, and their song, 'How Long?' which reached no 3 in the USA charts. They hoped that Cado Belle could follow suit.

It's all a bit of a dream-come-true. Here we are, out for a meal in a swanky Glaswegian restaurant. Anchor's boss in the UK, Ian Ralfini, and his artist and repertoire man, Alan Holsten, have flown up to Glasgow to meet us and to have us sign a recording deal. They are both charming, positive and upbeat about the band and its great potential. They present us with a gift, a bottle of Southern Comfort each, (presumably a nod to the Mississippi steamship). I am quite touched when Ian hands me a biography of the great saxophonist, John Coltrane. These guys seem to genuinely have faith in us.

One of my songs, Airport Shutdown, has been earmarked by them as a possible single and they are now scouting around for a suitable producer to take us into a studio to make our first album. Like spoiled kids we happily accept the gifts and the praise, too young, naïve and flaky to take in the full implications of our contractual responsibilities. Anchor supply us with a small weekly wage, not quite enough for us to live on, but with income from gigs added in, we can get by.

In December 1975 we headed down the A74 to test ourselves with the London audiences. We played many of the smaller music venues of the time, The Nashville, The Speakeasy, The Wellington and Dingwalls in Camden and received good responses from the audiences. This was our first stay at the Madison Hotel in Paddington. Here the accommodation was cheap. Dormitory style, we slept four to a room on skimpy mattresses. After a couple of days, we began to realise that The Madison was half hotel, half brothel. Call girls were booking in with their clients for an hour at a time in some of the upstairs rooms.

We returned to The Madison the next spring to do another run of music venues. In the daytime we were part tourists, part musicians, taking strolls through Hyde Park down towards Oxford Street. Once there we could pop into the Anchor Office and chat to staff.

One time a journalist from Sounds Magazine shows up at the office. Why has he chosen to interview me rather than other band members? This puzzles me until I see the paper the following week. The article is titled 'Tully-vision'. The journalist obviously couldn't get such a good pun out of the other band members' names. I show it to my mum and once again she has reason to feel proud. She even starts a scrapbook of her son's achievements.

Being in London gave us a chance to check out other bands. Our favourites were Kokomo, a joyful, celebratory nine-piece. They did a soul, R n B-type set and delivered a great show.

The band was fronted by three singers, Frank Collins, Paddy McHugh and Diane Birch who could do tight harmonies as well as taking lead vocal in individual songs. Maggie loved what they did and got chatting to them after gigs. I was in awe of the very mellow Mel Collins on saxophone and Alan loved Jim Mullen's 'Cornell Dupree' soulful guitar style. Although we could never match the big sound that they have, not to mention the talent, Kokomo became a new model for us to follow.

At The Madison one day we got to meet some musicians living in rooms upstairs. These were the drummer and keyboard player from a band new to us, 'Johnny Wilder's

Chicago Heatwave'. Sitting on the bed in their shabby hotel room they had a look of seasoned musicians who hadn't thus far climbed very high on the ladder of success. Nevertheless, I sensed a quiet and purposeful determination in the keyboard player, Rod Templeton, who mentioned that they had a single coming out soon. It was months later that I realised that Rod had been talking about 'Boogie Nights'. With the band's name now shortened to Heatwave, 'Boogie Nights' became one of the classic dance tracks of the seventies. Rod Templeton wrote the song and his talent as a song writer soon after came to the attention of Quincy Jones. Rod went on to write a host of disco classics for Michael Jackson, including 'Rock with You', Off The Wall' and 'Thriller'.

One time, whilst helping Simon load our equipment into a venue, a man with hippy garb and long, dark, curly hair appears on the pavement beside us. It doesn't take long for Alan to recognise one of his guitar heroes, Peter Green. He has a gentle but vacant air about him, like the lights are on but there's nobody in. We have a faltering conversation with Peter and invite him to come along to our gig but are somewhat shocked to see such a guitar-playing legend in this disturbing state.

I remembered as a fifteen-year-old being entranced by his distinctive, soaring guitar phrasing on Fleetwood Mac's 'Mr Wonderful' at the flat of my friend, Jim. With Fleetwood Mac, Peter Green went on to write and perform a series of distinctive chart hits for the band: 'Albatross', 'Oh Well', 'Man of the World' and possibly his most well-known track, later covered by Carlos Santana, 'Black Magic Woman'. Sadly, by the time we ran into Peter in 1976 he had suffered from years of psychotic episodes after taking LSD and had been in and out of mental hospitals, sometimes being subjected to electro-convulsive therapy. When we met him, he was still in a delicate state of mental health. It is good to know that he did eventually make a recovery and went on to play and tour in various bands for a couple of decades.

When in London, Alan Holsten, Anchor's A and R man, would take us all out for the occasional 'pep talk' curry evening. In a curry house in Chelsea, he broke the news that a producer has been found to record our first album and was flying over from the States to catch us at a gig. Keith Olsen was unknown to us but we soon learned that he was a big fish. He was the guy responsible for putting Stevie Nicks and Lyndsey Buckingham together with the original Fleetwood Mac, producing their No.1 selling eponymous album in 1975 and thus launching the career of one the most successful bands of the late twentieth century.

It's summer 1976 and the band is ensconced in a beautiful old vicarage in the depths of rural Pembrokeshire. Our hosts are hippy escapees from London who, like many others in the early seventies got out of the rat race and bought into the alternative 'good life' to be had in West Wales. As a means of generating income, they provide the perfect environment for bands to rehearse with minimal distraction. We have set up our equipment in their soundproofed barn and can practice whenever we like. Vegetarian meals are served up as well as access to a comfortable lounge with a cool vinyl collection. Courtesy of Anchor we have two weeks of this luxury to help us prepare for the recording studio. Keith Olsen, who has agreed to produce us, is showing up on the second week.

One day, a mate of our hosts makes an appearance at the Vicarage. He is Nick Turner, sax player from the celebrated space-rockers, Hawkwind, best known for their hit single, 'Silver Machine'.

It's a surreal moment for Gavin and I. Some five years earlier, aged sixteen, we had gone to a gig in London at a venue off Trafalgar Square and had seen Hawkwind performing. We were somewhat unimpressed with the band in spite of the massive volume coming out the PA system and the trippy ether-lamp light projection.

Given our tender age we were no doubt more entranced by the statuesque Stacia dancing naked at the front of the stage. Stacia was a Hawkwind fan who would jump up on stage, get carried away by the music and, bit by bit, remove her clothes. She was later invited by the band to join them as a front of stage performer She has said in interviews that her behaviour was not meant to sexual, rather an expression of the liberation brought on by Hawkwind's propulsive, acid-edged music.

Nick, the epitome of deep hippiedom, tucks his long golden locks behind his ears and leans forward to the kitchen table to roll a joint. 'Thai grass' he reverently announces, flaking bits off a mustard-coloured lump of hashish into the carefully-glued cigarette papers. 'Good stuff' he continues respectfully, lighting the bulging joint and passing it around us to be shared like a communal sacrament. As with alcohol there are many choices available in the varieties and preparation of hashish. I have never come across Thai grass before and am curious to try something new. The joint finished, Nick suggests we go into the barn and play some music together. By the time I've walked the 100 yards to the stone barn I'm feeling decidedly strange. Once I'm in the building, the possibility of playing my saxophone appears much too complicated and I sit myself behind Davy's drum kit. I pick up a pair of felt beaters and experimentally create a roll on his crash cymbal. Suddenly the visual part of my brain is overactive and the reverberation of the cymbal morphs into a giant ocean wave which in my mind's eye is breaking onto a long sandy beach. Intrigued, I proceed to create more 'waves', engulfing myself in shimmering cascades of sound. Suddenly I am pulled out of my reverie by a dissonant attack of notes. Nick, lost in his own private universe, is honking like a goose, disturbing, angular phrases coming at me from the bell of his saxophone. What he is doing is no doubt as meaningful to him as my oceanic cymbal strokes are to me. Sadly, we are now alien beings from different parts of the universe unable to communicate in the same language. Overwhelmed by the giant gulf between us I put down the beaters and walk out, leaving Nick to carry on with his inscrutable imaginings.

Keith turned up a few days later. I remember feeling decidedly underwhelmed, disappointed even, by his contribution at this stage. I had expected him, like some university music professor, to take our tunes, re-organise their structure and shape them into something better than they currently were. Instead, he listened to us play through the songs and made very few suggestions. We knew we were under pressure to produce at least one single from this forthcoming album, a single that would not only establish our wider reputation but also generate enough income to refill Anchor's coffers. However, Keith was very chilled and mellow and seemed worryingly content to accept the arrangements of our songs as they were.

His producer's mind must have been working to some extent, however. After he'd been with us for a couple of days John, our manager, took me aside and told me that Keith wanted to put strings on one of Stuart's songs, 'That Kind of Fool' and a couple of my songs, 'Stone's Throw from Nowhere' and 'Rocked to Stony Silence'. He wanted me to come up to London with him to meet string arranger, Paul Buckmaster.

Two days or so later, Keith and I are rolling through the patchwork fields of the Welsh countryside towards the English border, Anchor Records happy to furnish a chauffeur to take us the considerable distance from Pembrokeshire to Paul Buckmaster's Chelsea flat.

Paul has a well-established reputation by this time, having contributed valuable orchestrations to famous recordings such as Leonard Cohen's 'Songs of Love and Hate' and David Bowie's 'Space Oddity', not to mention his work with Elton John. Arriving in his flat he immediately appears to be a consummate professional, wasting no time before getting down to work. On listening to the demo recordings, he pulls out a large sheet of manuscript paper, spreads it on the floor and, with his pencil and ruler starts working, plotting out the sections of the songs and spontaneously humming and sketching down potential lines for the string players. We only stay an hour or so but before we have left, his orchestration is already well under way.

As our chauffeur takes us back to our far-flung Welsh vicarage, I settle into a pleasant state of anticipation. Soon we'd be in the recording studio. With Keith's production knowledge and Paul Buckmaster's string arrangements we'd at last be able to bring our collection of songs up to another level.

Arcadia 1970

Ronnie at Mugdock
Castle 1970

Ian Fergus and his
personality cult

Mugdock rituals and music

My band 'UP!' Woody, Gavin, Jim, Me Posing in our DJ's 1974

Cado Belle West Highland Tour, from left Alasdair, Me (misery guts),
Maggie, John, Stuart, Alan, Jim Wilkie, Davy and Simon

Cado Belle 1976

Me and Gav

Maggie in full flow

Gavin, Stuart, Alan, Maggie, Me and Davey

VICTORY in THE HAGUE. The Dutch had seen
nothing like these wild scenes of jubilation since
Dana sang our first Euro winner in AMSTERDAM
ten years ago.

Johnny and I arriving back in Dublin after winning Eurovision

Stagalee 1980 Me, John, Honor, Errol, James and Tommy

Tina gets the party going

Sensorium - Duncan,
Henry, John Paul, Paul
and Me

Nuadha Qaurtet - Carles, Me, Pedro and Chris

# 7 Proving Ourselves

*'There's always this sound out there that's just a little beyond my reach and that's just what keeps me going.'*

*Bill Frisell*

Summer of '76 was so hot and dry that the grass turned varying shades of brown and yellow. Even the trees were struggling in the drought and the leaves in their uppermost branches withered. For two weeks in the midst of this heatwave we were locked-down in a recording studio in Chipping Norton, Oxfordshire, laying down the tracks that all our hopes were to be pinned on.

Keith insisted that a drum 'riser', a hollow stage platform, be built. This he said, would significantly improve the overall sound of the drum kit. The construction of the riser took two days by the end of which we 'greenhorns' were champing at the bit, desperate to get on with the project. When we finally began to record the songs, things went smoothly enough. We knew our material inside out and Keith wasn't asking for any major alterations to our arrangements. Once the basic tracks were completed it was time to add backing vocals and horn arrangements. We saw this as a chance to bring in musicians from our favourite band at the time, Kokomo. Maggie invited in the singers whilst I brought in Mel Collins to perform horn arrangements with me.

Stuart's song 'Rough Diamonds' is probably my favourite track on the album. Mel and I laid down both flute and saxophone lines. I then asked Mel to take a solo on his soprano sax. I didn't have a soprano sax at the time and it seemed like the best instrument for the mood of the song. Mel didn't disappoint and within a couple of 'takes' effortlessly produced some haunting melodic lines over the song's coda.

Keith certainly knew his trade as a sound engineer. The drum riser did produce a rich and resonant drum sound. To achieve the optimum quality on Alan's guitar solo on 'Rocked to Stony Silence' he suggested that Alan play his guitar solo in the toilet, the tiled walls producing extra resonance. Keith also introduced Alan to 'high string' guitar when the bottom three strings on the guitar are tuned up an octave producing a silver-toned bell-like quality, reminiscent of a twelve-string guitar.

After two weeks the job was done. In reality we were too close to what we had created to properly evaluate it but we finished in a positive frame of mind thinking that we'd done a good job. With Paul Buckmaster's string arrangements still to be recorded and overdubbed and with the final 'mastering' of the tracks by Keith it would surely be even better.

A few weeks later the band is gathered together in a friend's flat in Glasgow. Excitedly we handle the first copies of our album. The cover shows a daft photo of the band made to look like we are on a large billboard in a London

Street. Above the billboard is a large neon sign advertising 'Cado Belle', the lettering designed in an art deco style by our friend, Stuart Patterson. Beneath the billboard a tidal wave is rushing down the street and we are supposedly reacting in shock to the soaking that the passing wave has given us. To achieve the startled reaction to this wave had involved, a few weeks earlier, standing in a photography studio and having buckets of cold water thrown at us.

We are all there, John, Simon, our long-suffering roadie, and Alasdair, our lyricist, assembled around the hi-fi speakers. Everything is beautifully balanced and the recording is a faithful rendition of what we sound like. Paul Buckmaster's string arrangements are musical and lyrical, adding a new dimension to the three songs chosen for orchestration. Alasdair and Simon, who weren't in Chipping Norton to witness the recording process, are hearing the tracks for the first time and seem impressed.

I am still too close to the album to objectively evaluate its merits. One thing does emerge for me out of the listening; I am far from happy with the sound I am creating on the alto saxophone.

I have over my time so far with Cado Belle been under the spell of American sax player, Dave Sanborn, whom I first heard playing on an album with the Brecker Brothers, Michael and Randy. After releasing his own first album 'Taking Off' Dave Sanborn had quickly risen to prominence as the 'go to' alto saxophonist, gracing the recordings of many pop and jazz artists of the day, from the track on Jaco Pastorius' debut album, 'Come on, Come Over' to David Bowie on his song, 'Young Americans'. Sanborn produced a unique gospel-infused sound, distinguishable on hearing just a couple of notes. His passionate, bluesy runs would soar over a song, lifting the energy to another level. I had been doing my very best to emulate that sound. After a year of loud gigs with the band I had been blowing my sax so hard to the point that I was losing out on the whole rich palette of subtle timbre that the instrument is capable of. Once, playing in Tiffany's in Edinburgh, a talented jazz saxophonist by the name of Gordon Cruikshank took me aside and gave me the sobering feedback that I was sounding more like an electric guitar than a saxophone.

Listening again to Mel Collin's soprano saxophone on the album was a kind of epiphany. Not only did I want to turn away from the harsh forced sound I was producing on the alto I had also fallen in love with the liquid tonal possibilities of the soprano.

I am taking a tortuous bus journey across the central belt of Scotland, my destination being a chicken processing plant going by the name of 'Chunky Chicken', on a mission to purchase a second-hand soprano saxophone from an employee of the factory. Being at this time a committed vegetarian, this feels a little like consorting with the enemy. However, my desire for a soprano saxophone is taking precedence over my considerations for animal welfare.

I am met in reception by the seller, his knee-length, white factory coat spattered with fresh blood stains. 'Would you like a quick tour?' This denizen of vegetarian hell seems friendly enough. Without bothering to wait for my response he leads me into a large room, the far end of which has double doors leading outside to where a lorry is parked. Men are busy unloading crates of live chickens from the back of the vehicle. The birds are quickly suspended upside-down on a long moving conveyor belt some six feet high above the floor. Clucking and squawking, they dangle from the moving belt before being dispatched by a revolving blade which decapitates them. Granted, this is a quick death for the birds but the factory scale of the slaughter I find depressing. I inwardly renew my vegetarian vows.

'I'm on my break', my host announces. 'Would you like some lunch?' An image of processed chicken nuggets quickly forms in my imagination. 'Err, I've brought my own' I answer weakly, as he leads me to the cafeteria. Munching my cheese and pickle sandwiches amongst the Chunky Chicken staff I try not to focus on the carnage evident on their overalls. After we've eaten, my host disappears briefly before returning with the saxophone casually held in a carrier bag. 'Sorry it's not in a case' he apologises, removing an ancient old horn from the bag and placing it on the dining table. Saxophones often have a protective lacquer coating. If this one ever did, it has long since disappeared. Vert-de-gris is apparent in some corners between the key-work and the bottom B flat key sticks out at a worrying angle.

He wants eighty pounds for this antique. I paid less for my beautiful Selmer alto. I pick it up and handle the keys. I don't want to risk blowing it. Goodness knows what germs might be lurking in the mouthpiece. Apart from the wonky B flat key everything seems in place. I decide to go for it. After all, I've come such a long way. I hand him the cash and, carefully cradling my new possession, I flee from the factory of death.

My new saxophone scrubs up nicely. I have some leaky pads replaced and the wonky key sorted. It turns out to have come from a French manufacturer by the name of Dubois in the late 1920s, the beginning of the jazz era when sales of saxophones rocketed. The old metal alloy from which it is made gives it a rich mellow sound and I now have a new colour in my musical palette.

We are in The Usher Hall in Edinburgh to witness the musical phenomenon that is Weather Report. They are doing a European tour and rumour has it that Joe Zawinul, their Austrian-born keyboard wizard is introducing each concert by performing an extended improvisation on a folk tune associated with the country in which they are performing. He doesn't disappoint. With his arsenal of keyboards, he takes us through a symphonic rendition of 'Ye Banks and Braes'. This could have come across as 'cheesy' but Zawinul initially treats us to in a rich exploration of harmonic movement, summoning up the effect of a whole orchestra improvising together before he introduces fragments of the tune on his mini-moog, the melody rendered plaintively and heart-felt.

Weather Report is a jazz supergroup. Their blend of world jazz has won them many admirers and the hall is packed. For musicians of the time, they represented a whole new model which has huge resonance even today. When their bass player Jaco Pastorius ripped the frets out of his bass guitar to create the first fretless bass guitar, it was nothing short of a revolution for bass players, and that, coupled with his extraordinary playing technique, places him as one of the towering figures of jazz in the last century. Their music, delivered at rock concert volume is a carnival of celebration, driving and rhythmic but often lyrical. I hear Wayne Shorter squeezing lullaby tones out of his soprano saxophone, once again confirming for me the expressive possibilities of the instrument.

In London, some of us go to watch Stephen Spielberg's 'Close Encounters of the Third Kind'. At the climax of the film, the actor Richard Dreyfuss, as the film's main protagonist, Roy Neary, plays a musical phrase on a synthesiser to the aliens on board the 'mothership'. The aliens repeat the phrase back to him, thus establishing a channel of communication. When I heard the joyful celebration of life that is 'Birdland', the opening track on Weather report's album 'Heavy Weather', I formed the fanciful idea that if our planet was ever visited by aliens and wished to communicate with us through music then I would nominate Weather Report as the best representatives of human culture.

Cado Belle's performances began to reflect the jazz end of the musical spectrum. Instrumentals influenced by The Mahivishnu Orchestra or the Latin jazz of Airto Moreira began to appear in our set. Davy was up for this, being a Mahivishnu and Billy Cobham fan and Maggie was happy to wing out on a Flora Purim-influenced 'scat solo'. Whilst this injected a bit of excitement into our performances it was, looking back, a distraction from what Anchor wanted from us, the elusive hit single.

A few weeks after we had finished the Chipping Norton recordings Alan Holsten booked us into a London studio and hired Glyn Johns, the well-respected engineer/producer. Glyn had engineered or produced countless artists: Bob Dylan, The Beatles 'Get Back' sessions and more recently Joan Armatrading's 'Love and Affection'. Alan hoped he could hone our recording of

Airport Shutdown into something more likely to succeed in the singles market. Sadly, the session achieved nothing more than increasing Alan Holsten's frustration, Glyn unable to get us to flex what we had achieved with Keith Olsen. Anchor went ahead and released Keith's recording of the song, which predictably skirted around the wrong end of the charts for a couple of weeks.

The gigs kept coming, providing a modest income as we drove up and down the country promoting the album. Anchor organised a support slot on a national tour with the Scottish songwriters, Gallacher and Lyle, hoping that the exposure to new theatre audiences would raise our profile.

Gallacher and Lyle had achieved much success with their memorable songs. They had explored the art of songwriting over the past ten years creating hits for Art Garfunkel with 'Breakaway' and their own hits 'I Wanna Stay with You' and 'Heart on your Sleeve'. (The Graeme Lyle song 'What's Love Got to Do with It' would later become Tina Turner's biggest hit of her career in 1984). Perhaps Anchor also hoped that some of their song writing skills would rub off on us.

For the duration of the tour, we have turned our back on the hired van and are travelling in style in Gallacher and Lyle's luxury tour bus. Across the corridor Graeme Lyle is removing his headphones. He has just been listening to, in one go, the whole of Stevie Wonder's long-awaited double album, 'Songs in the Key of Life' and is looking emotionally overwhelmed. Apparently moved by Stevie's song-writing skills he shrugs his shoulders and mutters rhetorically in disbelief 'How does he do it?' Accomplished and memorable as Graeme's songs are he knows Stevie's writing is on another plane.

Further down the bus and engrossed in the book, 'Supernature' by Lyall Watson is Jimmy Jewel, the band's alto saxophonist. Jimmy becomes another sax-playing inspiration to me, producing a clear golden tone on his horn. He played the graceful solo at the end of the above-mentioned song, Joan Armatrading's classic 'Love and Affection'. In the Albert Hall, for our final concert of the tour, I catch Jimmy in the dressing room and confess to him that I'm on a mission to improve my sound. 'Try this', he says, pulling a bakelite mouthpiece out of his case. 'It's yours for a fiver'. I ditch my metal mouthpiece with which I had been striving to sound like Dave Sanborn and replace it with Jimmy's bakelite one. It produces a softer, more rounded tone. I haven't used another mouthpiece since.

Cado Belle has a gig at the prestigious Glasgow Film Theatre. This is a bit of a feather in our cap as it's not every day that we are headliners, playing to a seated theatre audience. I had mentioned to my parents that the concert was coming up but was rather surprised when they announced they would like to come. My mother's scrap book of her son's career was filling up with newspaper articles and photographs on the band so perhaps they felt they had better go and see what all the fuss was about. We have a decent enough turnout and play what we think was a tidy set which receives generous applause. I go to catch my parents before they leave, naively expecting them to pour praise on our performance. Their response takes me back with surprise. They were appalled by the volume, especially the drums which my father considers 'an awful racket'. 'It's just not music at all!' my mother blurts out, looking at me in a perplexed and concerned manner. I feel for a few moments that I have betrayed the musical values with which they had brought me up; all those years in the choir; my Bachelor of Music degree. They leave the theatre hurriedly, no doubt desperate to get back home where they can set fire to my mum's painstakingly built-up scrap book. Looking back, I should have put them off coming. I should have known the generational divide was just too great. Many older people of their generation had embraced popular music, accepted that The Beatles maybe 'had something', had maybe danced a little to pop music at a wedding disco but my parents, for better or worse, had kept their musical tastes firmly in the past, a time placed safely before the rock and roll revolution of the fifties.

Alan Holsten has one last idea to raise Cado Belle's prospects higher than endless tours of the university circuit. At one of our curry house rendezvous', he gently but firmly puts across the idea to us that we do a cover of someone else's song. We are in no position to go against his idea. Long lists of possible songs are debated over but eventually a plan emerges. We are to make a four track EP. Alan is hoping that at the very least one of the tracks might prove a winner.

Track 1. 'Gimme Little Sign'. A song performed back in '66 by Brenton Wood'

Track 2 'It's Over'. A song written and sung by Boz Scaggs

Track 3. 'Play It Once for Me'. A new song by Stuart and Alasdair.

Track 4. 'September'. Essentially an instrumental by Alan but with a sung verse added by Maggie.

We are in a suite of studios in Notting Hill with Muff (brother of Stevie) Winwood, in the production chair. The band, Queen, are recording in one of the other studios. We sneak upstairs and through a little square pane of soundproof glass in the studio door, we observe them in the middle of their recording process. Brian May, his mass of curls tumbling over his face like a displaced eighteenth-century periwig, is refining a guitar track. Over and over, he repeats a high-pitched sequence of notes at ear-splitting volume. It makes for tedious listening but there is something impressive about his determination to go the extra mile for that perfect take.

To my ears the songs for our EP emerge from the session as being bland and devoid of innovation. Apart, of course, from Alan's tune, 'September'. This is a slow ballad which shows off Alan's tastefully exploited ability to sustain notes at high volume on the edge of 'feedback' (Feedback for the uninitiated: if the sound produced when the guitar goes over a certain volume and the guitar is pointed towards the amplifier then the note will distort in an 'interesting' way, typically leaping up an octave or another higher harmonic.)

We are told some weeks later that the new Cado Belle EP has got into the hands of 70's dance-hit wizards, Earth, Wind and Fire. Apparently, they were impressed with 'September'. We began to speculate, rather optimistically, that they might do a cover of it. No version of Alan's song appeared, but the biggest dance hit in Earth, Wind and

Fire's career, released in November '78, at least shares the same name, 'September'.

Stuart, Maggie and I are in a pub in Quilty, Co. Clare, on the west coast of Ireland. Having failed to find a telephone box we have asked the man behind the bar to help. First of all, he has to call the operator and exchange some polite banter before he asks to get put through to the garage. Then more banter with the garage owner before he gets around to the point of the call. "Well now. We have some folks whose van's broke down." The accent is as thick as a slice of soda bread. "Here, now. I'll just be passing you over". He hands the heavy, ancient phone, possibly of pre-war design, to Stuart who does battle with the garage owner's accent. Nothing moves quickly in the west coast of Ireland. "Looks like we're here at least until tomorrow", announces Stuart as he hands back the telephone to the barman.

It's a beautiful place to be marooned, after all, people come to small seaside villages like Quilty for their holidays. The only slight pressure is we have a gig in Dublin in a couple of days. What if the repair takes even longer? The concerns that we have chosen to come on a sightseeing trip in the middle of the Cado Belle Irish tour, are quickly put to one side as we settle into the hospitality offered by this very traditional Irish pub. The locals are curious about the new arrivals. Over a pint of porter, I get chatting to one, a thick-set man, on the right side of middle age and wearing an ill-fitting dark suit that may have been handed down from his father. He introduces himself as Joe. Joe has made an early start on the porter and now, placing his third pint on the table he feels has achieved the right quantity of Guinness in his blood stream. From an inside pocket he pulls out a tin whistle.

The previous year back in Glasgow, Alan and I had gone to see Stanley Kubrick's three-hour epic period drama, 'Barry Lyndon'. This was our first exposure to the music of The Chieftains whose music is part of the film's soundtrack. The air, 'Women of Ireland' by Sean O Riada, is the film's main theme, plaintively rendered on fiddle and whistle. The beautiful shaped melody made a big impression on Alan and I and we later practised it up, Alan evoking all the song's melancholy effectively on the sustained guitar tones he had mastered so well.

When Joe began to play his whistle, I felt I was in the presence of an authentic living tradition, music passed down the generations, something that the rest of the UK has largely lost and Ireland has still retained in its culture. After he had given us a few tunes I plucked up the courage to take out my soprano sax. I had a thin repertoire of Scottish jigs and reels, mostly learned from my father and I played a couple of these for Joe. He was impressed, probably not so much with my playing, but more with the sound of the saxophone. He seemed spellbound by the instrument and when we left him later, he told us he'd be saving up to buy one just as soon as possible.

We booked ourselves in for bed and breakfast in a rather grand old house. In the evening, we were encouraged to spend time with an old matriarch who was resident there. She was quite a character and a fount of knowledge on Irish culture. Amongst other thing she was an authority on genealogy and on hearing my surname, pronounced that the Tullies were in ancient times, physicians to the High Kings of Ireland, an association I could only feel flattered by. On hearing that we were musicians she requested a song. It may sound now like a poor choice, perhaps rather clichéd, but when Maggie sang 'Danny Boy' it sent shivers up my spine. Her naked, unaccompanied voice seemed perfect in that setting and she sang with a poignancy and depth of feeling that I had never heard in her Cado Belle repertoire. I felt in those moments intensely moved but also proud to be associated with her. The old lady enjoyed it too and was prompted to tell us the story, surely just a myth, that the melody for Danny Boy was sung by the fairies to a man returning home late one evening from his local pub.

After our sojourn in the Celtic Fringes, we returned to Dublin where Davy, Gavin and Alan had been sampling the culture there. We found Davy in a bad old state, his head wrapped around with a bandage, looking, like Maggie said at the time, like 'Mr Bump'. Having enjoyed perhaps one or two drinks too many at a nightclub he had fallen down a flight of stairs and bashed his head.

After passing through the entrance gatehouse to Trinity, Dublin's University, you find yourself in a series of interlocking courtyards laid to lawn. It was when we were walking through one of these courtyards that we first heard Errol Walsh and his band 'Stagalee'. On hearing the music drifting through one of the doorways we went in to the room to have a proper listen. We were all impressed with Errol's singing and the funky attitude of the players. What we didn't realise then as we watched and listened that the seeds were being sown for the notion that Gavin, Maggie and myself should all, in turn, emigrate to Ireland.

# 8 The Steamship runs out of Steam

*'Music is your own experience, your own thoughts, your wisdom. If you don't live it, it won't come out your horn.'*

*Charlie Parker*

April 1978. Jim Wilkie has put a short tour on for us. Again, it's the Highlands and Islands. We look forward to a few days in the sticks. Driving through the romantic glens of the Scottish Highlands we could almost pretend we're on a holiday. Few of us, however, have properly considered the implications of the itinerary. There is a slight problem; Jim doesn't seem to have scheduled in any time for sleeping.

Firstly, we play in Aviemore, Scotland's famous ski and winter sports hub. In April the snow has largely melted, and the venue is quiet. In good spirits, we try out a couple of new tunes in our set and enjoy playing together. When the performance ends, we load the van and set off, driving through the night to Ullapool, the West Highlands port, to catch the early morning ferry to Stornoway. Jim, anticipating that the good people of Lewis will be enthusiastic to hear us and firmly turning a blind eye to our earlier experience on the Isle of Islay, has booked us to play both an afternoon and an evening show. Fortunately, the two audiences that show up are welcoming and appreciative. The only problem is that after playing two shows we are beginning to get a bit punch drunk with tiredness, sleep the previous night having been a couple of dozing and head-nodding hours in the van between Aviemore and Ullapool. By the end of the evening, we are exhausted and dragging our feet. It is now necessary to drive down through Lewis and into Harris to the port of Tarbert, where we are to catch the overnight ferry to Uig in the Isle of Skye.

As Stuart switches on the engine, it comes to his attention that the van is very low in diesel, with not enough to get us to Tarbert. Petrol stations are closed at this late hour and we are advised to head to Stornoway's harbour. Here we manage to blag some diesel from one of the fishing boat owners. Unfortunately, this has to be siphoned from a plastic canister through a long tube. Stuart volunteers to do this and gets a mouthful of diesel for his trouble. We reach the Tarbert ferry in time where once on board, Jim has assured us, we will be able to sleep. Theoretically he is right but unfortunately the crossing only lasts a couple of hours. No sooner have we lain ourselves out on the uncomfortable benches in the hope of getting some shuteye and it is time to be on the move again. We stumble into the van and drive onto Skye. Skye is a large Island and to travel from Uig to Broadford where beds and blissful sleep await is still another tantalising ninety minutes of driving. As we wind our way across Skye's treeless landscape in the early hours of the day I watched Gavin beside me, the most miserable I had ever seen him in my life, his head slumped forward, weeping with despair.

By 1978 our hatred of the A74 has reached a new level. Each journey south begins with two hours on this road, a dual carriageway, often peppered with road works before we reach the English border where the M6 motorway, with its luxury of three lanes, begins. The A74 has an infamously high number of traffic accidents and we are becoming cynical Scottish nationalists, suspicious that Westminster doesn't care about the fate of Scottish motorists.

Much has happened since we first travelled down this road filled with optimism for our first run of gigs in London at the end of 1975. Now the dream of success and wider recognition for the band is slipping away as the weeks and months slip by. Recently, we had been invited out by Anchor for a meal in London's Chinatown. Ian Ralfini, boss of the Anchor operation in the UK is there as well as our patient A&R man, Alan Holsten. I haven't seen much of Ian since the time, two years before, when he and Alan flew up to Glasgow. He was, back then, full of optimism for the band's future. Now that previous incarnation of himself has evaporated and he looks anxious and worried. It seems that the good ship Cado Belle has finally run onto the rocks and Anchor can no longer bail us out. The 'noodles in hoy-sin sauce' have gone limp and lifeless in my bowl. I can't help feeling disappointment and some responsibility that in spite of all the opportunities given to us we haven't made a success of things.

The release of our EP did little to change our fortunes. Friends said we'd been unlucky, telling us we'd been eclipsed by the arrival of Punk. We started to wonder if our polished and produced sound was now out of fashion. The Sex Pistols, The Rezillos and The Clash with their raw, high-energy performances were fronting an attack on the carefully produced, mid-Atlantic approach that the likes of Cado Belle epitomised.

On one occasion, recording for BBC radio at London's Maida Vale studios we ran into an all-female punk band, The Slits. With their messy hair and anarchic vibe, they symbolised a new anti-establishment mood sweeping through the music industry. It would have been easy for us at that point to conclude that we had become the establishment and were not politically attuned to the times. Ultimately, however, it is all down to the song. Whether the song is punk or mainstream, that elusive formula of catchiness and accessibility has to be there. That was truly what eluded us and to blame our failure on the arrival of punk is all too convenient.

The year after we had recorded our album in Chipping Norton, Gerry Rafferty booked himself into the same studio to record his second solo album 'City to City'. As the recording progressed one track emerged head and shoulders above the rest. 'Baker Street' was in itself a piece of pop music artistry; aching melancholy over soulful chord movements with a melody that's sits easily in the memory, but when the iconic sax riff was added to the mix the song was destined to become a classic. The fact that at the time the Sex Pistols and The Clash were turning heads was immaterial. Baker Street just had to be a success no matter what was going on in popular culture at the time.

Unfortunately, Cado Belle had no 'Baker Street' up their sleeves.

Somewhere on our travels we pull over in a lay-by on a quiet 'B' road. The sun is shining and after some considerable time cooped up in our hired transit van, we are happy to spill out and stretch our legs. Somebody has a 'beat box', a massive lump of moulded plastic with stereo speakers housed at either side and an audio cassette player mounted at the front. Somebody slips in a cassette of Steve Miller's 'Fly Like an Eagle'. This mellow hippy anthem kicks off with a funky Stratocaster riff before the Hammond swirls and chops its way over the drum and bass groove. Cosmic looping synthesiser evokes the feeling of another dimension. Something strange is going on. Is it our sense of being released into the warming sunshine after being stuck inside a van for three hours? Is it that for a few moments we just want to be carefree and forget that Cado Belle has not been the great success we hoped it would be? Is it the joint that Simon has just rolled and passed around? Who knows? Whatever the reason, Steve Miller's 'Fly Like an Eagle' has the band dancing around the beatbox, laughing and smiling, oblivious to passing motorists, just for a few moments catching a glimpse of some former state of innocence.

*'I'm going to fly like an eagle, to the sea*
*Fly like an eagle, let my spirit carry me'*

I had a girlfriend around this time named Alison. She had been a student at Stirling University and after graduating continued living in a country estate called Cromlix, just a few miles from Dunblane. She worked for the owners and shared a flat, former estate workers lodgings, with Norman, who was doing a post-graduate course at Stirling. In my gaps between Cado Belle gigs I would travel up to Cromlix to spend a couple of days with them. The estate, with its grand house and gardens was a beautiful environment to hang out. It was sold off in 1981 and became a luxury country house hotel, now owned by tennis star, Andy Murray. Back in the late seventies Alison, Norman and I would play part-time aristocrats, going for walks up into the local grouse moors, boating on the private lake, but most of all playing long games of Frisbee on the lawn or nearby fields. In the evening we'd eat very well before settling down to listening to music, enhanced by what Norman called a 'post-prandial' joint.

Alison and Norman had befriended a couple who lived in a converted stable at Cromlix. These were Robert Lewis and Vashti Bunyan. Occasionally we would all go for a drink together in Robert's battered old car. In the pub one evening Robert disclosed that Vashti had made an album back in the sixties. 'It was quite good', he enthused. Unfortunately, it didn't sell well'. Vashti appeared painfully shy with the subject of her earlier career being brought up, leaving Robert to do most of the talking. Bit by bit, as I got to know them, snippets would emerge of the now well-known story of their year-long journey from London to the Outer Hebrides by horse and wagon to join a commune being formed by their friend, Donovan. "By the time they finally got there, Donovan had abandoned the idea," added Robert, wistfully.

The iconic gypsy wagon still lay in the yard outside their converted stable. The romantic journeying life had inspired Vashti to write a collection of songs which became her first album, 'Just Another Diamond Day', produced by Joe Boyd. Discouraged by poor sales Vashti turned her back on the music business in 1970, to raise her children. However, in the early noughties her songs began to circulate on the internet and the song 'Diamond Day' being used in a TV commercial, re-launched her career, thirty years later.

Back in Glasgow, in July 1978, John announced that Cado Belle had a gig coming up in the Music Machine in London. We would save money, he suggested, if we didn't bother to book a hotel and drove straight back home after the gig.

The A74 beckons us again. We repeat what has now become a familiar ritual. Somebody has volunteered to pick up the van from the hire centre. This was either John, Stuart or Alan as they have current driving licences.

We all help to load up the equipment into the van. This comprises:

*PA system (several large speakers and a mixing console,)*

*Backline; guitar, bass guitar and piano amplifiers.*

*Boxes of cables, box of microphones. Box of microphone stands (very heavy).*

*Drum kit. Electric piano, guitar and bass guitar in flight cases. Saxophones.*

Simon expertly supervises the packing into the back of the van, a three-dimensional jigsaw puzzle. Then we head off, Maggie sitting at the front, her knitting needles clacking away above the rumble of the engine and Dill the dog resting on the seat beside her. The rest of us occupy the seats behind, sometimes chatting, sometimes nodding off. A couple of service station stops for coffee and sandwiches, a run for the dog. We eventually crawl into London some seven hours after leaving Glasgow, park up outside the service entrance to the gig, stir ourselves out of our torpor and carry the equipment into the venue. Simon gets on with positioning the PA system and wiring everything up. The rest of us bring in the back line, assemble mic stands whilst Davy pulls the various drums and cymbals out their cases and sets up his kit. An hour later we're ready for a sound check. Time for a quick meal at a local restaurant. Back to the dressing room to put on stage clothes, have a beer, get psyched up to play. Check set lists. An hour and a half later we're done. Fifteen minutes to wind down, chat to one or two fans or friends who pop into the dressing room. Audience has now left so it's back onto the stage to dismantle everything and put things back into their cases. An hour later we are once again loading the van. Half an hour later we're off, Simon requesting how he needs some food as he missed out on the meal earlier. We slip out of London and join the motorway, stopping at the first service station, to feed Simon. The motorway is quiet but monotonous so somebody must sit by the driver to keep him awake. Somewhere just North of Penrith Alan is at the wheel when he nods off. The van lurches across a couple of lanes before Alan is prodded awake and disaster avoided. 7.00am and we're back in Glasgow and unloading gear into our various flats. The unlucky driver is not allowed to go to bed but has to drive the van back to the hire company before walking home to get some long-awaited sleep.

The tide has finally gone out for Cado Belle and The Music Machine is the last gig the six members play together.

The vacuum created by the Cado split is quickly filled. Jim Wilkie has written a bunch of songs and asks us to record them with him. We spend a few happy weeks at Brian Young's Ca-Va Studios, now relocated to a St. Vincent Street basement, putting down backing tracks and having a creative time with overdubs. All of Cado Belle are involved and we have a chance to rub shoulders with other musicians; Blair Douglas, the accordion player from Skye and Kim

Beacon who contributes backing vocals. It becomes a labour of love, Brian Young and ourselves willingly putting in the hours. At the end of the day Jim has a tidy album with some strong songs but it fails to attract record company investment. Another victim of the punk revolution, perhaps.

Alan has gone to seek his fortune on his own in London, quickly finding work with Steve Harley's Cockney Rebel. Gavin has headed off to Ireland to join Errol Walsh's band, 'Stagalee'.

I'm not sure what Stuart is up to at this time but he has very generously left his Fender Rhodes piano in my bedroom. Whether it was through altruism or for his convenience, I'm not certain. It certainly turns out to be very convenient for me when I get chatting to a young film director by the name of Bill Forsyth at a party in the flat. One of my flatmates, Mick Coulter, is a cinematographer who has been working with Bill and has invited him along to the party. Bill has been making a film, 'That Sinking Feeling' with some young actors from a youth theatre and Mick has suggested to him that I might be interested in writing some music for it. Without much else going on in my life at the time it's too good an opportunity to miss. A few days later I'm looking through the film with Bill, plotting out where he'd like music placed. I head back to the flat, sit myself down at Stuart's piano and the ideas start pouring through me.

A few weeks later I'm back in Brian Young's Ca-Va studio, now based in St.Vincent Street. I'm in the company of two great musicians, Alan Taylor on bass guitar and Kenny McDonald on drums to lay down the soundtrack for the film 'That Sinking Feeling'. The film follows the adventures of a group of unemployed youngsters who set about improving their fortunes by raiding a stainless-steel sink factory. The spoof drama demanded a 'cops and robbers' feel to the music. Since I had imbibed a fair amount of American crime series, Kojak, Columbo etc. as a teenager in the early seventies, it was second nature for me to reflect that in the writing. Alan and Kenny worked well as a rhythm section and contributed much to making the music authentically 'gangster'. As for me, I had a great time finding my way with the Fender Rhodes and overdubbing occasional lines with my 'Chunky Chicken factory' soprano sax.

That Sinking Feeling was a regional success in Scotland but didn't at that time stir up much interest south of the border. The strong Glaswegian accents perhaps being indecipherable to some English viewers. As far as I knew that was my film-score-writing career over and I turned my attention elsewhere.

I put together a few songs. The ideas for melody and song form came easily to me. The lyrics I quickly scribbled down, being perhaps too easily pleased with achieving rhyming couplets rather than digging deeper and finding something meaningful to express. I booked Ca-Va Studios and asked my friend, Terry Neason to sing them. I ended up with four songs to hawk around the London record companies.

Shortly after, I ended up in London receiving the generous hospitality of my Glaswegian friends, Ian Parker and Brenda Arnott. I had befriended Ian and Brenda some years earlier before they moved down to London. They rented a large house behind a shop in Wandsworth into which they welcomed all kinds of waifs and strays like myself. Their open and welcoming attitude to people made their house a kind of hub, especially for musicians and creatives. Ian was a musician and was often out playing gigs all over London as a keyboard player. Brenda was the house matriarch who would sit at the table and entertain us with her stories and sharp wit. Downstairs there was a basement kitted out with a drum-kit and electric piano which Ian used to rehearse his current projects. Abstract paintings created by a Scottish artist friend hung on the walls of the living room where we'd sometimes sit in the evening listening to a variety of albums from the likes of Viv Stanshall to the French progressive rockers 'Magma'.

I stayed with Ian and Brenda for several weeks, making appointments with artist and repertoire people from various record companies regarding the songs I'd recorded. One of them thought that a song, 'You Brought Out the Best in Me' was perfect for Dusty Springfield. "She hasn't been active for years and this could be the song to relaunch her career", he mildly enthused. "I'll make sure she gets a copy". Needless to say, I heard nothing more.

Ian and Brenda's house operated like a utopian commune. They were very open-minded and, on a mission, to knock down traditional barriers. It was Ian who proposed I should take some LSD. He told me that he liked to take a 'trip' every few months himself, to stop him from becoming too fixed and set in his ways. A few days later a young woman arrived with some 'tabs' of LSD. I did have reservations about taking the stuff. John, the manager from Cado Belle had done a trip which he had described as 'walking along a tightrope with sanity on one side and insanity on the other'. The memory of that comment didn't exactly fill me with the confidence to go ahead, but Ian assured me it would be fine and the young woman told us it was 'good quality stuff'.

The majority of the trip I spent in Ian's rehearsal basement. Like my experience with Nik Turner's Thai grass, I entered a deep state of wonder. With the LSD there was an even greater appreciation of the potential beauty in everything. Ian had a Fender Rhodes piano in the basement. I spent quite some time playing chords on the piano which I imagined were launching out into the infinite space outside the room. Different combinations of notes hung and shimmered in the air with a quality of exquisite beauty. Of course, anybody listening would probably have thought my playing was quite boring but my brain was tuned into a very different perception of reality. It was all very benign and peaceful with, thankfully, no bouts of paranoia or worry. It gently wore off but for a couple of days after the trip I felt quite different, more positive and outgoing.

When I returned to Glasgow, Stuart, never short of a fresh idea, decided to reform Cado Belle with a different line-up and do an Irish tour. We had toured there two times already with the original line-up and had always had a positive reception from audiences there. I was very happy to tag along. That the tour was a success is perhaps incidental to the flow of events. Perhaps more important was that we again met up with Errol Walsh and Stagalee, advancing a connection that would lead Maggie and I into a new phase of our career.

# 9 A Year in Ireland

*'The music is not in the notes but in the silence between.'*

*W. A. Mozart*

I'm in a pub in Coleraine, County Antrim in Northern Ireland. The publican has given out the call for 'last orders'. Some canned music comes through the pub speaker system. I recognise the familiar opening phrase of the British national anthem and people all around me are rising to their feet. Instinctively, my inner rebel takes over and I decide to remain seated. Back in Scotland nobody bothers to stand for the national anthem any more, and it's been years since I've heard it played at a public gathering. Errol is nudging me with his elbow as he rises. 'Stand up Colin, for God's sake' he mutters out the side of his mouth. Tommy, across the table, is also mouthing 'Stand up' to me. Bemused, I reluctantly come to my feet. When the music finishes and the noise of chatter has resumed throughout the pub Errol explains the gravity of the situation. Had I not stood up my behaviour might have been noted by loyalists, who might have thought nothing of 'doing me over' outside the pub later as I was leaving. We are in the era of 'The Troubles' in Northern Ireland and allegiances are carefully observed. It could have been bad news for me to have been seen as a republican sympathiser.

The day before, my new girlfriend Anna, Maggie and I had set out on this new adventure. The Cado Belle dream had finally evaporated after our last Irish tour so when Errol gave Maggie and I the call to come to Ireland to join forces with his band we had nothing to lose and perhaps plenty to gain. We knew the music scene in Ireland was vibrant and a living could be made from playing music in a band and touring the circuit. Anna and I had only been seeing each other for a couple of months but she too was happy to come along for the adventure of living in another country.

Errol had been fronting bands for years, playing guitar and singing but he was keen to let Maggie take over on lead vocals. He had gone through various personnel for his bands, including Gavin on bass who, the previous year, had joined Errol for a few months. Errol had recently recruited a fantastic drummer, John Forbes, who loved his status of being the only black man (with the possible exception of Thin Lizzie's, Phil Lynott) living in Dublin at this time. James Delaney on keys and Tommy Moore on bass were seasoned players having paid their dues with various Irish line-ups. Stagalee played funk-rock and here was a level of grit to it that had been lacking in Cado Belle, a sense that these guys were just into the music without chasing some big dream of international success. Essentially both Cado Belle and Stagalee looked to America for their musical influences but the fact that Ireland was geographically and culturally slightly closer to the UK seemed to make Stagalee's approach more authentic. Errol gravitated towards the music of 'Little Feet' and particularly admired a musician by the name of Little Beaver. A song of his, 'I can

Dig It, Baby' regularly appeared in the Stagalee set. One of Errol's tunes, 'Give a Little Love' had been released as a single the previous year and had earned Stagalee a positive reputation in the Republic.

Errol, Maggie, Tommy with his girlfriend Maeve, myself and Anna squeeze ourselves into a three-bedroom, semi-detached rented house on a suburban estate on Dublin's north side. It is a totally inappropriate dwelling for a band intent on noisily rehearsing and partying on a regular basis. It doesn't take long before the neighbours hate us and our landlord is coming around, begging us to leave.

Fortunately, the band has by this point rehearsed up its songs and we are ready to go on the road. With its reputation already established we quickly pick up gigs. Soon we are in an enviable position of making a comfortable living on three or four gigs a week, driven around the country by our roadie, Arlow, in his Mercedes van. We are free spirits; no record company is pressurising us to become more 'commercial' and we are able to follow a musical direction of our own choosing.

In Ireland at this time there was the phenomenon of showbands; - bands who would tour the circuit but, in our eyes, had sold out by pandering to popular taste, playing chart songs and old Elvis tunes. On our nocturnal journeys returning from the likes of Limerick or Cork, we would sometimes see a van carrying a showband and there would be an excited exchange of horn toots, as we kindred creatures of the night acknowledged each other. I remember feeling a certain arrogant pride that we played our own music and hadn't sold out like them.

Dublin in the late seventies struck me as having a very different character from cities in the UK. Perhaps what distinguished it most was its lack of high-rise buildings. I never came across a building taller than five storeys. Just like the Clyde dissects the city of Glasgow, the River Liffey divides north from south creating something of a demographic demarcation. I began to appreciate in time that south Dublin was, generally speaking, more affluent with more traces of the city's colonial past being apparent: Georgian architecture in the squares and Trinity College with its grand quadrangles. One grey damp day when crossing O'Connel Bridge I was shocked to see a young boy, perhaps four years of age sitting on the pavement in the drizzling rain, in front of him the limp cardboard lid from a Kraft cheese slices packet containing a couple of coins. It was a pitiful sight. I later learned that this was a ploy to arouse maximum sympathy and revenue by travellers who had been forced to beg since the dark days of the Irish famine.

Extracting money from passers-by was something I myself was not averse to trying. Anna and I moved into a shared house in Monkstown, an area well to the south of the centre and closer to the port of Dunleary. It wouldn't have been fair on our neighbours for me to practise the saxophone in the house so I would sometimes take myself off into the centre of Dublin to go busking. One of my favourite busking pitches was a lane off Grafton Street, around the corner from the famous Bewley's Tearooms. Opposite me was a church and with Ireland having a mostly devout population at this time there were a fair number of people going in and out. I became convinced that entering the spiritual atmosphere of the building rendered people more charitable. On leaving the church they would often toss a few coins into my case as they passed. That fact, coupled with the resonant acoustic quality offered by the narrow lane made this a perfect busking spot. I allowed myself to get lost in the music, letting rip with a full sound. But then I made a classic misjudgement. With a continuously passing trade, I figured I could get away with playing the same tune several times in a row in order to really perfect it. Nobody would notice. They would only hear ten or twenty-seconds of the music as they walked past. Unfortunately, I didn't calculate on the staff working in the Bewley's kitchens above me. They certainly did not enjoy hearing the same tune several times in a row, played at full volume. Their displeasure was expressed in the form of a large saucepan of cold water being emptied over me. Half shocked, half embarrassed I dripped off home, deciding that was it for the day.

Stagalee, a name associated with the 'wild west' bad guy, became out-dated with Maggie now on lead vocals. A friend of Errol's suggested we rebrand ourselves as 'The Pumphouse Gang', counter-culture characters from a sixties Tom Wolfe story. Errol and I put a song together called 'Welcome Back into my Life' which we recorded at Windmill Lane Studios in Dublin. This got released under the name Pumphouse Gang on the 'Little Black Records' label and picked up a good amount of radio play in Ireland.

I was at this time approached to play saxophone with a singer unknown to me by the name of Johnny Logan. He had a song written by Shay Healey called 'What's Another Year' which was being entered for the national heat for the

Eurovision Song Contest. I was initially sceptical of having any connection with a competition which I considered a bit of a joke, a competition that brought out the cheesiest elements of the pop music industry. But curiosity soon got the better of me and I agreed to get involved.

Firstly, I met the affable Johnny. Son of a well-known Irish tenor, Patrick O'Hagan, he seemed perfect pop star material, young and handsome with oodles of Irish charm. Shay, the song's writer, worked in RTE, the Irish equivalent to BBC. He had been writing songs for some time and was a performer in his own right. 'What's Another Year' was dedicated to his dad. His mother had died the previous year, the sentiment of the song being that his father's life was now empty and pointless without his wife being around to share it with him.

Shay, Johnny and I went to meet the song's arranger, Bill Whelan. We didn't know it then but Bill would go on to create the global phenomenon that is 'Riverdance'. Bill had studied law at university, his parents perhaps not being too positive about their son's first choice of career; to be a musician. How misguided they were. On graduating from university Bill immediately turned his back on his prospects in the legal profession and pursued what was to become a very successful career as a composer and arranger. At his house we listened as he sketched out his ideas on the piano for his orchestral arrangement of What's Another Year? His ideas elevated Shay's song to a new emotional level, the arrangement reminiscent of Jimmy Webb's 'Wichita Lineman', sung by Glen Campbell back in '68. The resonance of the saxophone motif in Gerry Rafferty's 'Baker Street' was probably going through Bill's mind when he gave me the phrases, he wanted me to play over the song's introduction. As for the saxophone feature in the song's middle and on the coda, he gave me the freedom to improvise my own lines.

To win the Irish heat and to find that we were going on to the contest's final took us all by surprise. Having initially been hesitant about getting involved with Eurovision I now couldn't help getting swept along with the glamour of it all. To play to a potential of 400 million people around the world was frankly, mind-boggling and would take some nerve to see it through.

We are in The Hague for the Eurovision final in April 1980. Team 'Johnny Logan' has now swollen to include Johnny's manager, Louis Walsh; Shay; the three female backing singers; Noel Kelehan the song's conductor; Johnny's brother, Mike and various others tagging along for the Eurovision ride. Back in the seventies there was a long-running TV advert for the Woolwich Building Society which had the catch phrase 'No, I'm with The Woolwich!' Some bright spark in Johnny's management handed us out pink T-shirts which we were all encouraged to wear. Printed on the front of the T-shirts in large lettering was the tasteful phrase: 'Fuck the Woolwich, I'm with Johnny Logan'.

On the evening before the contest Johnny, Shay, Mike and I took ourselves out for a meal in The Hague's city centre. There was much exotic fare on offer; we opted for Vietnamese; a cuisine not yet seen on the streets of Dublin. After the meal we strolled around town. Aware of the relaxed approach to cannabis in Holland, Shay and I were on the lookout for somewhere to score. We effortlessly picked up some hash from some people outside a youth centre. Back at the hotel we tried the stuff out. I retired to my hotel room feeling distinctly odd. This hash was stronger than anything I've hitherto experienced and I found myself compelled to lie on the bed contemplating with some considerable rising panic that tomorrow I would have to perform to the largest TV audience of any show in the world. As I descended into a vortex of blackness another even more pressing concern took over: after smoking this joint there seemed a frighteningly real possibility that I might well never wake up again.

One of the good things about smoking hash is that unlike with drinking alcohol, you don't wake the next morning with a hangover. After a good night's sleep, I was completely recovered from my Dutch hashish encounter. And a good job too. The excitement in Johnny's entourage was building as we contemplated the day ahead over breakfast. It certainly was going to demand focussed attention.

Later that morning we all arrived at the 'Nederlands Congresgebouw'. By modern Eurovision standards it would probably appear to be a moderately sized performance space. Back then, looking out from the stage to the rows of tiered seats it appeared absolutely massive, certainly the biggest auditorium I'd ever performed in. Every country had a slot for an on-stage rehearsal accompanied by the large pit orchestra. After spending years squeezing onto small stages with Cado Belle and Stagalee the stage in the Cobgresgebouw seemed disproportionately large. Johnny, myself and our three backing singers were distantly far-flung from each other as if we were performing during a covid-19 outbreak and were taking socially distancing far too seriously. I could just make out the alto sax player in the orchestra. He gave me a reassuring thumbs up after he heard my opening lines, just what I needed in this intimidating environment.

The day passed in a kind of blur. So many performers were milling around in a state of adrenalised anticipation. I remember observing the UK's entrants, 'Prima Donna' rehearsing in one of the rooms backstage. They epitomised everything I feared about the Eurovision phenomenon; a formulaic cabaret act of two pretty young couples, kitted out in matching pink and blue outfits with tightly rehearsed dance routines under a smarm of fake smiles and gestures. I looked at my black jeans and scruffy black shiny bomber jacket and felt a tad guilty that I hadn't made more effort with my appearance. No wardrobe mistress had ever approached me to discuss what I should wear. At least Johnny was making an effort with his spotless white suit and black shirt. He even had a matching black scarf draped conveniently over his right shoulder, in case I suppose, he took a chill during the performance and needed to wrap up.

Coming onto that vast stage was surreal, Johnny seated at the front in the centre, the backing singers seemingly a good tennis court's distance away from me on the other side of the stage. My Dutch sax player friend again gave me a big smile and another thumbs up as my top teeth found the top of the mouthpiece and I prepared to play those opening notes. The conductor, Noel Kelehan, lifted his baton, gave the downbeat and we were off. Once I'd played the fanfare-like phrases of the song's opening section I could relax into the experience. To play with a live orchestra was a privilege I'd never had before, nor indeed, have I had since, and I wanted to be as present as possible, soaking up the whole atmosphere of the event. Johnny was a total professional and delivered the song faultlessly. His dreamy, 'Prince Charming' good looks probably had millions of teenage girls, not to mention middle-aged women swooning in front of their television sets. His final falsetto leap in the last phrase, 'What's another year?' sent a slight shiver up my spine. I knew by then we were in with a good chance of winning.

Looking back, I can now see that the song's strength was born out of the genuine emotional response that Shay felt for his father's loss. That original emotion was sufficiently channelled by Johnny as he performed, giving the song an integrity that is seldom apparent in a Eurovision entries.

Once the performances were complete it was back to the 'green room' where all the performers congregated for the second half of the evening, when they would be allocated points from the various competing countries. We watched the points come in on a large screen. Screams and group hugs abounded for the next hour as the 'douze points' came in. When he realised, he had won Johnny was, quite rightly, ecstatic. Super-charged with adrenaline he bounded onto the stage raised his arms above his head in a triumphant gesture before taking the Eurovision cup, kissing it before proclaiming 'I love you Ireland'. Mr Eurovision, as he later became known, had scored the first goal of a Eurovision hat-trick which he'd complete in 1992 when he wrote the winning song.

Every Eurovision winner is guaranteed to generate singles sales across Europe. 'What's Another Year' did particularly well, becoming number one in the pop charts in nine separate countries. Johnny's management saw my saxophone contribution as part of the act and offered me the chance to tour Europe, doing mainly TV shows. For the next few weeks Johnny, his manager, Louis Walsh and myself hopped on and off planes, lived the pop star life of being chauffeured to champagne receptions and were wined and dined lavishly by TV production companies falling over themselves to have Johnny on their show.

It was shortly after winning in The Hague that the song reached number nine in the British charts. This necessitated an appearance by Johnny and me on Top of The Pops. My thirteen-year-old self would have been astounded. The following week it was the British Number one. To play on the number one slot on Top of The Pops surely would have been a feather in my cap. However, I had other plans; Anna and I were getting married in Glasgow on the day TOTP was being filmed. Johnny's management found another sax player, Paul Duffy to stand in for me.

For the next two or three months as I was away in Europe every few days with Johnny and the ebullient, irrepressible Louis Walsh, enjoying the champagne receptions and staying at five-star hotels. Anna was by this time five months pregnant with our first daughter, Nuala.

Meanwhile, changes were afoot in The Pumphouse Gang. Maggie was restless and perhaps felt her career wasn't developing the way she would like it to. She quit the band and headed back to the UK. It wasn't long before she was working and touring with Mike Oldfield, eventually producing the evergreen classic, Moonlight Shadow, in 1982.

The band reverted to their old name, Stagalee, and recruited a new singer Honor Hefernan. I did a few gigs with them when I was back in Dublin. I wrote a couple of songs at this time, opportunistically hoping that they might earn a place on Johnny's forthcoming album. I booked a studio and got the Stagalee musicians in to record them with Johnny on vocals. The guys did a great job and I was well pleased with the tracks. Johnny was non-committal, being perhaps too much under the guidance of his management who preferred him to follow mainstream blandness. It is interesting that given his status as Eurovision winner, his subsequent releases failed to chart. When I was in London with Johnny, we met up with Cliff Richard's producer and played him my two tracks. He seemed to like them and made positive noises. In the end, however, one he thought was too funky and the other the lyrics were not good enough. Johnny on hearing this verdict lost interest in the songs. My opportunistic bid had failed.

It was James, the keyboard player from Stagalee who took me aside before a gig at the Baggot Inn. He asked me a straightforward question, 'why did I consider the commercial potential of a song to be so important when I was writing?' I was initially a bit taken aback by his question but on reflection was grateful for his comment. It was true that when I was putting a song together, I was tailoring it for some imaginary audience, the lyrics submitting to some common denominator of public taste. I'd like to think that my writing at the time was more edgy and original than songs manufactured for Eurovision but yes, I have to admit I was being seduced by the possibility of revenue from chart success. Before the Baggot Inn gig James presented a song of his to the band, a kind of old-fashioned, honky-tonk tune. The song was very much an expression of his personality with lots of quirky character. He was being entirely faithful to his own taste and I had to admire his integrity.

One of my last gigs with Stagalee took us over to the west of Ireland. It was a very friendly, casual affair, almost like a folk club out in the sticks. I can't remember if we stayed over, it being quite a distance from Dublin but I do remember Errol after the gig sitting in a lounge with the people that had invited us to come and play. He had an acoustic guitar and was taking requests. It was then that I realised that Errol had another string to his bow in the form of a large country music repertoire.

Song after song he sang and he seemed to know all the lyrics. I remember thinking what a natural musician and entertainer he was and only later found out that he knew this repertoire from his teen years, learning these songs from his mother. I didn't know back then that he would go on to make two award winning country albums, one of them in Nashville.

Back home Anna was probably wondering if she'd made the right choice by getting married to a musician who was always off gigging. She never said anything to that effect but I guess it must have often crossed her mind. Meanwhile she was more concerned with getting prepared for the birth of our daughter.

Our time in Ireland was coming to an end. My old Alexander teachers, Jeanne and Aksel, were starting up a training course for teachers at Dartington College in Devon and I had written to them to let them know I'd like to start the training. I was still deeply interested in Alexander technique and was happy to walk away from all the music connections I'd made in Ireland and start anew. I didn't really feel part of the show business package surrounding Johnny, and Eurovision had run its natural course. It was, however, a wrench to be leaving Stagalee.

My last gig with the band was shortly before the birth. It was at a hotel in Bray, a little coastal town just south of Dublin. Perhaps it was the acoustics of the room or maybe the band was playing too loudly but after the gig my ears were ringing. Being beautiful summer weather Anna and I borrowed a tent and went back to Bray to camp for a couple of nights. Anna was almost full term so we took our time climbing up onto Bray Head where we pitched our tent. The quiet of the place made me more aware of the constant ringing in my ears and I felt confirmed that I'd chosen the right time to be turning my back on playing in noisy bands. The tinnitus gradually lessened and we enjoyed a peaceful couple of days. With views out across the Irish Sea toward the UK mainland it felt like a fitting end to our time in Ireland.

Nuala was born on the 31st of August 1980. Shortly afterwards we threw a farewell party in our flat for all our Irish friends and Nuala, just a few days old, was passed around all the young women, eager to hold the precious new-born bundle.

A neighbour gave us a lift in his car to the ferry in Dunleary. How we managed all our belongings onto the ferry I can't imagine; suitcases, saxophones, backpacks, a newborn baby, not to mention the Hohner Clavinet keyboard I was clutching under my arm. James had kindly passed it on to me, a parting gift. It would prove to be very useful.

# 10 The Bucolic Life

*'Jazz washes away the dust of everyday life.'*

*Art Blakey*

Anna and I could not have dreamed of a more radical contrast to our life in Dublin. In September, 1980, I rented a cottage for us in the sleepy village of Harberton, a village which had grown quietly over the centuries around its mediaeval church, hidden away in a hollow at the end of single-track lanes that wound their way down from the main road south from Totnes to Dartmouth. Opposite our front door apple trees were dropping their windfalls onto the grass tussocks of a small orchard. The village, evolved long before the innovation of cars, was a woven web of interconnecting lanes, some only suitable for walkers, others barely wide enough for a horse-drawn cart.

Along one of the leafy lanes leading from the village I would, four mornings a week, take the three mile walk into Totnes to join the Alexander Technique training school. I didn't resent having to walk this distance and as the musty aroma of fallen leaves filled my nostrils on those autumnal mornings I could fleetingly be transported back to my teenage obsession with Tolkien's Middle Earth.

After college I would load my backpack with supplies from Cranks, the health food shop in Totnes high street and wend my way back home. Johnny Logan and Eurovision had provided us with enough money to see us through these first few months of the Alexander course and I felt reasonably confident in my new role as father and provider for my family. Looking back, it was an idyllic existence: my investment in a training which I felt was doing me good and, for the time being, experiencing the luxury of not having to earn a living. My need to play music, however was always there and I began to sniff around for playing opportunities.

The first band I was seduced by around this time were The Lizards. Already half-formed when I became involved it was a collective of local musicians of varying abilities and experience who produced a self-penned fusion of funky jazz that went down very well at the local pubs. The Dartmouth Inn at the bottom of Totnes was our favourite haunt and we could regularly pack the place with a crowd drawn from local party animals swelled by students from the nearby Dartington College. I felt justified in investing time with The Lizards; I couldn't resist the chance to blow my horn, revelling in those moments in the limelight, enjoying that sense of being someone who was doing something interesting. And, after all, there was a modest fee to be collected at the end of the night. However, with weekly rehearsals and poorly paid gigs it was ultimately a self-indulgent enerterprise for me.

As the months went by my bank balance began to dwindle. When Danny, one of my co-trainees on the AT course approached me about forming a band I saw it as a gift. It didn't matter that we'd be playing Country and Western, a style of music which I then considered hopelessly old-fashioned. Danny was confident we could pick up some well-paid gigs and given my need to start earning money, that was good enough for me. Saxophone was obviously out of keeping with the genre so I suggested I could play the Hohner Clavinet keyboard which James had kindly bequeathed to me on our departure from Ireland. By creating a swelling effect with the volume knob, I could, with partial success, emulate the sound of a pedal-steel guitar. Danny was our singer and guitarist and very much the band leader. He had learned his craft in the pubs of Glasgow and had memorised a huge repertoire of tunes from Johnny Cash to Gordon Lightfoot. He also had an equally large fund of jokes which he would entertain us with as he drove us to gigs in the likes of Dartmouth or Paignton on a Friday or Saturday evening. George, one of our fellow students played fiddle and Danny's son, Scott, given his tender age of fifteen, coped ably on the bass. Sometimes Danny's young daughter, Carol, would join us if we were playing locally in Totnes. She, like her brother, had been groomed by her dad in the country and western traditions from an early age and she would astonish us with a rendering of the likes of 'Words' by the Bee Gees, which dripped with a kind of second-hand, world-weary pathos copied from someone at least twice her age.

Danny came up with a name for the band, 'The Directors', a name which, devoid of any Country and Western overtones, puzzled most on first hearing it. It was Danny's 'in' joke and needs some explanation. A student of the Alexander Technique is encouraged to develop the skill of 'sending directions', a process whereby messages are sent from the brain to the neuro-muscular system to encourage lightness of movement and freedom from unnecessary tension. Ideally, this a process that goes on when we are in activity, be it hoovering the floor, taking a walk or lifting a heavy weight. Of course, as keen AT students we could try to maintain this awareness when playing music. Our efforts to produce lightness of movement and freedom from excessive tension in our performances doubtless flew over the heads of the inebriated audiences at the pubs and clubs we played but I found myself enjoying playing with this band and in spite of my initial judgement of the genre I found myself warming to the home-spun simplicity of the music. This was music for the people whereas I could see that the funky jazz we were aspiring to with The Lizards leaned towards virtuosity and self-indulgence. Having said that, The Directors did have one number which allowed George, our fiddle player, to show off his skills. This was 'The Orange Blossom Special' which told the tale of a violin player who engaged in a duel with the Devil to see who could play the fastest. I've no doubt we occasionally strayed into 'excessive tension' delivering this high-speed barn-stormer, especially the normally shy and reserved George, who would work up a bit of sweat as his bow flew across the strings.

I was still ensconced in Harberton when Bill Forsythe got in touch. He had contacted me when I was in Ireland telling me that he had a new film in the pipeline and was keen for me to produce some music for it. He wanted to play me the 'rushes' of his new film, Gregory's Girl, and plot out the various scenes where he felt music would be appropriate. We had a spare bedroom in the cottage in Harberton and I invited him to come and stay for a couple of days.

Anna and I were at the time creating our own version of 'hippydom', embracing veganism, raw foods, seed sprouting and low impact lifestyle. We were hopelessly devoid of technology. We didn't have a car and I had yet to get around to passing my driving test. Television was too mainstream for us so we chose not to have one. Video players were probably available but we were blissfully unaware of that possibility. In order for Bill to show us the film I had to ask Tina, one of the AT students on my course, to help out. Her husband was a drama lecturer at Dartington and had all the kit necessary for us to watch the film.

It was interesting to have Bill stay with us. He was easygoing and mild-mannered but capable of delivering the occasional flash of wry humour you would expect from the creator of such carefully observed films. After uncomplainingly chewing through his breakfast of sugar-free muesli, Bill drove us into Totnes where we spent the day at Tina's house watching Gregory's Girl and plotting out places where we felt music would enhance the unfolding plot. In keeping with my current low-tech lifestyle, I used the second hand of my watch to measure the approximate length of each section and scribbled the timings down on a bit of paper along with a brief description of what was happening in the scene. If Bill was disappointed in my lackadaisical, amateur approach he never let me know. We must have watched the whole film through twice by which time I felt I had mapped out all the places where music was going to be added. With no video player at home this session with Bill was my one and only chance to get familiar with his creation. In the evening we returned to Harberton where we fed Bill with our best vegan fare, probably something along the lines of buckwheat topped with beansprouts in a miso and tahini sauce. It had been a long day and Bill, somewhat disappointingly, chose to retire to his guest room soon after supper perhaps finding it difficult to find common ground with our alternative lifestyle. I was pleased to find a point of connection when I noticed as he left us that he was clutching a book which I'd recently read; Alan Ereira's 'The Heart of the World', a fascinating account of the Kogi people of Colombia. Perhaps there was a bit of hippyness in Bill after all.

When I had written the music for Bill's previous film, 'That Sinking Feeling' I had the luxury of being able to conceive and evolve the musical ideas on the Fender Rhodes piano which Stuart from Cado Belle had generously deposited in my bedroom. With this new project the battered Hohner Clavinet which I'd been playing with Danny's band had to suffice. Its set of strings was mostly complete but keeping the individual strings in tune was no easy task. I had picked up an amplifier somewhere, a VOX AC 30 as I recall, so I could at least play the keyboard at a reasonable volume.

A few weeks later I received a letter from Bill thanking us for our hospitality during his visit. I had to reach for a dictionary when he cheekily opened his message with the enquiry 'hope you are still enjoying the bucolic life'. In the letter were details of the schedule he had organised to record my music for the film. When I read that he'd hired Air Studios, one of London's top music recording facilities, for two days, the full weight of my responsibilities began to register more keenly.

I spent more time with the clavinet jotting down on manuscript paper a whole array of ideas I had for the score. I had by now visualised my dream band of musicians to play the music and excitedly phoned them to clarify whether they were available. My old Cado Belle mates, Alan and Gavin would be playing guitar and bass. I asked Ronnie, who was doing his music degree at Leeds College to play drums and percussion. Piano maestro, Ian Parker, who had accommodated me so often in his Wandsworth house was the obvious choice for keyboards and, in what was perhaps a rash moment of inclusivity, I invited his girlfriend, Brenda, to play the cello.

A few weeks later saw us all gathered in Ian's basement rehearsal space. I was in a rising state of adrenalised panic. Fortunately, the musicians were well up to the job and over a couple of days they brought my ideas to life in their own colourful way. It did become apparent however, that several years had passed since Brenda had last played her cello. She was very apologetic and would have been happy to duck out of the project but I encouraged her to stay with us, keeping faith with the old expression 'it'll be all right on the night'.

I had decided to play soprano saxophone on the recording sessions. During rehearsals I began to have doubts as to whether my ancient instrument rescued from the chicken slaughterhouse was good enough to record with. It was badly needing a service and some notes were playing out of tune. Having arrived in Air Studios I was suddenly seized by a last-minute panic that my dodgy soprano was going to ruin the session. Bill offered to hire me a better instrument and someone was sent out to retrieve one from a music shop. The expression, 'flying by the seat of my pants' comes to mind as I write this. How could I have been so disorganised? The hired soprano, fortunately, was immediately better but every musician knows that it can take a while to adjust to a new instrument.

The recording room at Air was generously proportioned. We all performed together and I don't recall any 'overdubs' being needed. The scenes from the film were projected onto a large wall at the back of the studio enabling us to time the music precisely. It was the first time the other musicians had seen any footage from the film and they were now more accurately able to attenuate their playing to suit the mood of each scene. After we had recorded a few sections, we went into the control room to listen to what we'd recorded so far. My adrenaline levels began to subside when I heard the music for the opening title scene. It sounded promising, the hired saxophone, mercifully, playing in tune.

A couple of months later Gregory's Girl was launched in a cinema in central London. There was a pre-launch gathering during which Bill took me aside to run through the financial options open to me regarding my musical contribution to the film. It was quite simple: either I took a straight fee or a percentage of future profits. I didn't deliberate over my decision for long. Based on the limited success of Bill's previous film, That Sinking Feeling, it felt reasonable to assume that Gregory's Girl would probably go the same way. I therefore accepted the fee they were offering, £750, which, at the time, I thought was a considerable sum.

It is best not to regret the decisions we make in life. Who could have predicted that Gregory's Girl was destined to become one of the most popular films of the twentieth century? It not only launched the new genre of Scottish cinema with many directors following in Bill's footsteps but also won a huge and enduring audience worldwide.

By training to become a teacher of the Alexander Technique I was creating a split in my career. On the one hand I was committed to finishing my training and establishing a teaching practice in something which I was deeply interested in and felt was of great value to people. But as Gregory's Girl accumulated plaudits and recognition friends would take me aside and ask me why I didn't build on its success and develop a career as a film composer. These comments I brushed aside. Alexander Technique was my main focus. Besides I've never been good at taking initiative and the idea of chasing up film directors and offering my services did not appeal. The bucolic life on offer in sleepy Devon held too much allure.

# 11 The Charms of Cloud Cuckoo Land

*'When I play, I think of how the phrases move as a dance, or something in nature like a bird or a shooting star.'*

*Don Cherry*

After the Gregory's Girl launch, I returned to Totnes and resumed the lifestyle I was developing there. In the summer of '81 Anna found herself a job picking strawberries which not only brought in some money but also as many strawberries as we cared to eat. We moved to a semi-detached cottage at Longcombe on the road from Totnes to Torquay, another slice of rural idyll in the rolling Devon countryside. Here Anna and I continued to embrace veganism and began to experiment with making non-dairy milk made from soya or oats. We also started sprouting alfalfa seeds and mung beans. In high summer with an orchard of fruit ripening next to the cottage, plum trees in our back garden and a regular supply of strawberries from Anna's employer, Charles, it was natural to go one step beyond veganism and to experiment with the idea of existing purely on raw foods. We bought large glass jars, the type you would find in old-fashioned sweet shops, in which to sprout the alfalfa seeds. In the warmth of the summer, we could produce a juicy crop within six days. With the mung beans we learned that they grow better in the dark so we cultivated these in the bath in a black bin bag where they achieved an impressive length worthy of a Chinese meal. In a spirit of vegan evangelism, I decided to scale up production and form a small sprouting company which we called 'Sprouts Unlimited'. I began to distribute these to local shops, Cranks, for instance, who had a restaurant at Dartington and a shop in Totnes High Street, taking a regular order. We also sold to friends. I found that the very health-conscious Alexander students of which, from September 1981, now numbered twenty were very willing to be supplied with our nutritionally-packed sprouts. As for existing purely on raw foods that phase didn't last more than a few months. I lost a lot of weight and after sufficient numbers of friends told me how skinny and off-colour, I looked, we went back to veganism.

Increasingly, we settled into the Shang-ri-la existence that's possible in South Devon. London, with its film industry contacts seemed another world away. Our neighbours at Longcombe, Jenny and Richard, had a toddler son, Solomon, an ideal little companion for Nuala. They were also of 'alternative' persuasions and Longcombe cottages became something of a hippy enclave. Richard ran up a 'skull and crossbones' flag on the pole on the corner to announce our little hippy kingdom to passing motorists.

There was a new book which espoused a new idea about child-rearing which had come into vogue at the time. This was 'The Continuum Concept' by Jean Liedloff. The book was based on Jean's study of an Amazonian tribe which she'd undertaken for her PhD. She observed just how relaxed and un-controlling the tribal parents were in their attitude to the safety of their children, for instance, allowing them at a very young age to handle sharp-bladed machetes. The Indians trusted that their children's intuitive instinct for self-preservation would keep them safe. Consequently, their children were allowed to explore and range freely within their environment and therefore develop more quickly into useful members of their community. Jean Liedloff proposed that parents in 'developed' societies were over-controlling and that the neurotic worries they projected onto their children hampered their natural development. Jean came to Totnes to give a talk about her ideas and Richard, Jenny, Anna and myself went along to hear her. What she said made a big impact on us. Later, I can remember having to hold back my desire to hold on to Nuala as she clambered herself up onto a delicately balanced chair, trying to trust she would not come to harm whilst my heart was still in my mouth. Richard excitedly recounted how he had watched Solomon, still a toddler, leave the 'safety' of a swing park and wander a couple of hundred yards off towards a nearby wood, all without once looking back for approval or reassurance from his dad. This, for Richard, was progress, an indication of what unhampered child-rearing should be like.

It was around this time that Richard introduced me to the music of American jazz guitarist, Pat Metheny. He had a vinyl of his latest album, 'Offramp'. I loved the sound-world Pat and his keyboardist; Lyle Mays created and became a devoted fan for years after. But it was another artist that Richard played to me that was to have even more of an impact. This was the Glaswegian singer-songwriter,

John Martyn.  After all these years I'm not certain which album it was that Richard played, but it was most likely John's much revered 'Solid Air'. I was familiar with a later album of John's, 'One World' which I'd got into in the late seventies but heard hadn't heard much of John's earlier stuff when he was more a purely 'acoustic' artist and was immediately intrigued and entranced in equal measure. As I listened to the tracks Richard played me, my earliest memories of seeing John, or Ian McGeechie as he was previously known, came flooding back.

I was four or five years old in Langside, Glasgow, playing outside in a deserted garden with some of my little mates when suddenly this older boy had appeared. Somewhat disdainfully he brushed past us younger lads and, placing his hands on the top of the garden's tall brick wall, gracefully pulled himself up. After showing off his climbing prowess he proceeded like a tightrope walker along the top. At the far end of the wall, he shot us a glance to check whether his audience was impressed before slithering down the other side and disappearing into the adjacent garden. After a few moments of respectful hush one of my friends informed us that this had been Ian McGeechie, one of the local 'big boys'. Move forward ten years. I was on a bus in my hated school uniform when a young man with tangled locks flowing over his hippy attire came onto the bus with a gorgeous girl in tow. They sat themselves opposite me, Ian's face alive with the sparkling wit with which he was entertaining his girlfriend.  Ian, McGeechie who had by then changed his name to the more internationally acceptable and infinitely more pronounceable John Martyn, was, of course, much too preoccupied to be aware of my presence but as I sat, sullen and embarrassed in my school uniform, my adolescent self-longed to be part of the world he represented.

Now, another twelve years later, I found myself listening to his music on a friend's record player in South Devon. His music had stood the test of time; 'Solid Air' having been recorded several years before still sounded cool, fresh, and heartfelt. I had been around music enough myself in the past ten years to be able to appreciate the richness and uniqueness of his voice and guitar style. John had been working, performing, and recording for many years, establishing a loyal and worshipful fanbase, but somehow, I had overlooked him. After immersing myself in that free-floating, scat-inflected sound for a few minutes I felt a deep connection. Whether it was our common Glaswegian roots or just the spell-binding quality of his music I am not sure, but I remember making an inner wish that I could play with him at some point in the future and contribute to that dreamy musical landscape he was painting; at last, to follow him over that garden wall to see what was on the other side. This mysterious universe we inhabit did in fact register and respond to my wish. I just had to be patient and wait three years for the wish to come true.

At the top of Totnes High Street is an old castle of Norman 'motte-and-bailey' design. The Norman castle is probably built on a fort of even greater antiquity, the elevation providing a good vantage over the surrounding area. People subscribing to the theory that the planet is criss-crossed with a system of earth energy lines, known commonly as ley-lines, would perhaps know that Totnes was on such a line, the crucial energy point being at the castle. In the 1980s this was one explanation offered up to explain why Totnes was such a magnet for all things alternative, liberal and 'left field'. Dartington Hall with its annual influx of new arts students added to the established population of writers, artists, musicians and practitioners of every wacky therapy imaginable. Whilst its cafes served up meals to cater for the growing number of vegetarians and vegans the bookshops offered up literature on everything from dowsing to Taoism, crop circles to self-sufficiency. To be a resident of Totnes at the time was to feel you were part of a quiet and secret revolution going on in sleepy South Devon, conveniently tucked away from all the major cities.

After living in the countryside outside Totnes for some eighteen months Anna and I were finally offered a flat above the Cranks shop in the Butterwalk, opposite the town square. We now felt truly at the centre of this emerging alternative community. We could buy all our vegan supplies, including delicious, freshly baked, sunflower seed loaves from the shop below and in return trade them our bags of alfalfa and mung bean sprouts.

It was then I was approached by a drama lecturer at Dartington to devise some music for a carnival procession he was planning. This was Peter Kiddel, a long-haired visionary who with his tall stature, broad-brimmed hat and long tailed-coat evoked the aura of a new-age wizard. Peter's speciality was creating thought-provoking events enacted in public spaces. I put together a band mainly recruited from The Lizards but also including a trombonist, Jim Fulkerson from the music department at Dartington. The music was simple, suitably carnivalesque, with a loping reggae backbeat. We processed up the long hill of Totnes' main street sounding like an under-rehearsed, slightly out-of-tune, banana republic band, shrill saxophones at the front and various Lizard percussionists following behind. At the very back the enthusiastic, rogue elephant trumpetings of Jim's trombone drove us on. Shoppers and pedestrians stopped in their tracks as we passed, beaming us smiles and with people hanging out of upstairs windows, cheering us on. It was a beautiful event and awakened in me a new understanding of the transformative potential of music and its role in the community.

Shortly after, I was again approached by Peter to compose some music for another event. A group of parents had turned their backs on traditional Christenings and yet wanted a way of publicly naming and celebrating their offspring. They had approached Peter to see if he could organise a naming ceremony and he and his partner, Cathy, the chance for Nuala to be part of this event.

On a warm summer's evening we found ourselves on the banks of the River Dart in the Ashsprington Estate. Firstly, the mothers arrived with their children by boat, having travelled the couple of miles along the river from Totnes. This journey symbolised the child's journey through the womb. After the mothers stepped off the boat onto the river bank, an event surely much less painstaking than giving birth, the process which it was meant to represent, they were met by the fathers who led them to the next part of this symbolic journey. On the grass under a grove of trees a maze had been laid out, representing the journey the children would be taking through life. At the entrance to the maze was a masked man. This was a kind of trickster figure who posed a riddle that had to be answered by the children before negotiating the 'maze of life.' Inevitably the children were too terrified by this masked character to answer his questions and clung tightly to their parents. Whilst walking the maze, a dreamlike atmosphere was created by our friend, Richard, who, in an extraordinary flouncy fairy costume was precariously perched halfway up a tree, launching wistful phrases on his flute into the evening air. Having successfully completed their walk through the maze the children had their names announced to the assembly of friends and family who responded with much cheering and clapping. By then I'd grabbed my saxophone and joined the band, launching into some celebratory music. We played a piece I'd written for the occasion named 'River Party' which featured several percussionists playing congas and shakers, a tune destined to be performed with subsequent bands I have been part of over the years ever since.

In spite of already being busy with The Lizards and The Directors my insatiable appetite for musical projects led to further involvement with a new band being formed by yet more of my fellow Alexander students.

These were Tim and Tasha. They were actually a married couple, a species of human not often found amongst my contemporaries who preferred less formal relationships. It seemed at the time that their marriage had recently foundered on the rocks yet they had enough love and affection for each other to play music together. They formed a band with me and our friend, Dyan, who played the congas. Tasha named us 'The Crazy Comfort Band', an apt enough name suggestive of the easy-listening, good-time 'Americana' in our repertoire. Again, I played my Hohner Clavinet. Dyan would stand behind us, driving the music onwards as he soulfully laid into his congas. He was at the time a 'Sanyassin', a devotee of Bagwan Sri Rajneesh. There was in Totnes a sizeable community of Sanyassins, easily distinguishable by the loose, orange-hued clothes they were encouraged to wear by their guru. They were known locally as 'the orange people.' They had reputedly been through a process of self-liberation brought on by breaking down traditional sexual taboos. This liberation seemed apparent in Dyan's approach to drumming which was wild, expressive and free, as if he were constantly in pursuit of an ecstatic state.

It was fun band with a lot of joyful energy going on. However, it was yet another example of me blindly feeling I had a right to have this kind of indulgent experience hanging on the thin excuse that I was earning a little bit of money for the family.

One day at the Alexander School, Jeanne, my teacher, took me aside and gently suggested that it was time for me to consider just how chauvinistically I was treating my wife. I was astonished to hear this from her. I saw myself as a man who was willing to share childcare duties and was handy in the kitchen. I felt I had a good relationship with Anna. We had the common interest of developing our expanding beansprout business. I felt Jeanne's comment was preposterous and unjustified, and thus remained absolutely myopic to the effect my ongoing involvement with the various bands was having on Anna.

A few months had gone by since the premiere of Gregory's Girl. It was now doing the rounds of the regional cinemas and I began to hear positive talk about the film and read reviews that were full of praise. I was still quite content to turn my back on the film's potential kudos dismissively deciding that the music I'd written was 'shallow' and not very interesting. I was now wanting to write and play music with more substance and beauty, something people might find interesting, uplifting, or even spiritual.

Ian Parker put me in touch with a music entrepreneur, Larry Page. Someone who Ian felt might put some money into a solo project of my own music. Larry certainly had the money and the connections but was ultimately an opportunist businessman. I was not sure of his background at the time but with a brief internet search I now know he had been working in the music business since the early sixties, managing bands like The Troggs and The Kinks. It is strange to think he had been present at the famous Troggs recording of 'Wild Thing'. I can remember walking round the playground, aged 10, with my little mate, Stuart, raucously belting out the chorus, the thinly disguised sexual charge of the song we'd probably heard on Top of the Pops the night before having made a big impression on us. As a kind of offshoot to his managerial career Larry had made several albums with himself as 'the artist'; 'The Larry Page Orchestra'.

When Larry cast his eye over my recent musical achievements, playing sax on a winning Eurovision song and writing music for a currently popular and successful film he must have felt he had a project he could run with. However, Larry's and my own ideas about the musical direction of any project could not have been further apart. To be fair, Larry did give me a platform to get some of my tunes recorded and allowed me to be the lead instrument. He hired another writer, fellow Scotsman, Callum Kenmuir, who would write some of the tunes, and then brought in an arranger to orchestrate them. The project all went ahead and a couple of months later I found myself in a sound booth in a large London studio. Through the glass in the main recording room were a dozen or so string players, and a rhythm section; Larry's 'orchestra'. We recorded the tunes swiftly and professionally with few re-takes, as I recall, and had everything done and dusted within two days.

Two months later I received a copy of the vinyl trough the post. The album was called 'Night Sky' and was by 'Larry Page and the City Sound Orchestra'. I'd no idea if I was given any credits as the sleeve notes were all in Japanese. On the back of the sleeve was a studio photo of Larry addressing the camera in his trademark outsize glasses, elegantly dressed in a white linen jacket with massive lapels, a gold chain bracelet on his wrist. I expect he was modelling himself on the likes of the successful German band leader, James Last. I was at a loss to see what musical contribution Larry had made to the project, yet, here he was presenting himself as a musical director. The album, it seems, was destined for the Japanese market. The album's titles, printed in English on the central disc of the vinyl, now dripped with sexual innuendo: I imagined Larry enjoying making them up: 'Let Me Discover You', 'Two as One', 'Once More', 'So Deep'. I had written a tune for my daughter which I somewhat unimaginatively but in a heartfelt way had called 'Song for Nuala.' On the album it was now titled 'Stay Awhile'. Any hope of producing music that was more uplifting, innovative, or spiritual went unfulfilled for the time being and I quickly reversed myself out of this experimental cul-de-sac, looking more to life in Totnes to fulfil my musical ambitions.

By the summer of 1981, my old mate from Glasgow, Ronnie, was winding up his music degree at Leeds College. His girlfriend at the time was Christine, one of the Alexander students in my year and on completing his course he came to Totnes to move in with her. He was keen to become musically active in the area and started making noises about creating yet another band. The Lizards were a loose collective of varying musical ability and Ronnie reckoned a new group, comprising Steve Lindon, the Lizards' keyboard player, myself, Ronnie and a new bass player, Dave Goodier, who had moved into the area could do some good things together. With all our energies and rehearsal time going into this new band which we somewhat arrogantly named 'The Flying Dragons,' a name that perhaps suggested we had sprouted wings and could now 'take off'. It wasn't long before the earth-bound Lizards ran out of steam, with some of our old band members no doubt justifiably deciding that we Dragons had done something disloyal and selfish.

In spite of the bad feeling we'd generated with The Lizards; the Dragons did enjoy a creative time together. Being a quartet rather than a sprawling nonet we found we had more space to flex our musical muscles. We could develop our writing skills and played instrumental tunes penned by Ronnie, Steve and myself. After a gig we were approached by a local benefactor who wanted to give us funding to record some of our music. This gave us the luxury of a couple of days in a London studio.

Recording is such an enlightening process. However, to be able to stand back and review all aspects of your musicianship is, to some extent, a risk; the recording may reveal the awful truth that what you are creating is not nearly as good as you had previously imagined. Conversely, when it goes well you can get a pleasant surprise and find you have even surpassed your imaginings. I think this session fell into the latter category. We were all high as kites after the recording and felt that what we'd achieved would turn a few heads. I certainly thought it was the best thing I'd done so far in my career. We were producing a blend of jazz instrumental music with nods to Weather Report, Brazilian music and the European jazz sound world of Manfred Eicher's ECM label. However, to make a living by becoming a recording artist in that world demanded a level of virtuosity and innovation which frankly was beyond us. We were followers rather than leaders. Perhaps if the band had stayed together and continued to develop, we may have earned that position through sheer perseverance and hard work. Sadly, it didn't work out that way.

In my last year of the Alexander training, on April 12th, 1983, our second child, Layla arrived. She was born in the living room of our flat above Cranks Food Shop.

It was around this time that Cathy Kiddel, Peter's partner, started taking saxophone lessons from me. She was very involved in Peter's work and often helped to produce his public ceremonies. She and Peter were an 'off-grid' couple and had even taken their son out of mainstream education. She was very enthusiastic about the potential of home education which in her opinion allowed children to thrive and reach their full potential. She had even written a published book about her son's experiences of being educated at home whilst they had travelled around the country with theatre groups. Anna and I were quite taken by her ideas and filed away the notion of home education for future reference. On hearing we had a new baby Peter offered us the chance to become involved in another naming ceremony he was planning.

In the summer of 1983, a collection of babies, toddlers and parents gathered at a pre-arranged spot-on Dartmoor. A pentagram had been marked out on the heath. Each point of the pentagram represented one of the Chinese Five elements: wood, fire, earth, metal, and water. Before arriving with the babes at the pentagram, Peter arranged for the men and women to process from different Bronze Age standing stones on the moor. When the men and women had converged near the pentagram music was played by a small band of brass and woodwind players. The music had been written by Peter's friend, Nick and was played before the parents led their children through the pentagram. Unable to resist the opportunity I had had also written something which we played after Nick's piece. Unlike the celebratory 'River Party' of Nuala's naming ceremony my piece was more sombre, perhaps reflecting that our time in South Devon was running out.

Steve Lindon, the Dragons hard-nosed, locally raised keyboard player came along with his partner, Heather, to both these naming ceremonies. He was somewhat bemused by these fanciful events and described life in South Devon at the time as living in 'Cloud Cuckoo Land'. He was probably right.

In the summer of '83, the first ten students from Jeanne and Aksel's Alexander Training received their teaching certificates on the lawn in front of Dartington Hall. Soon after it became apparent that our idyllic lifestyle in Cloud Cuckoo Land was coming to an end. Jeanne had organised a job position for me as an Alexander Teacher back in my hometown of Glasgow; an opportunity to join a thriving practice and start my new career. After paying out for my training and going through the course it seemed like the obvious next big step and that I'd be foolish not to take it.

It was difficult to leave behind all the friendships and memories we had built up over the three years. It wasn't without some misgivings that we packed up in September, said goodbye to Totnes and its many charms and headed north into what seemed, by comparison, a monochrome future.

———◆———

# 12 Childhood Hero

*'In the midst of creating, a person is raised to another level of consciousness that doesn't have much to do with everyday thinking. It's as if you could imagine life before there were words.'*

*Charlie Haden*

It's the summer of '84, 11:30 pm and I'm driving back to Glasgow up the A74 after a performance in the border town of Dumfries. I should feel elated as I've just completed my first gig with John Martyn: the wish I made three years earlier in Devon finally did come true. It was everything I hoped it would be. I'd managed to carve out a place for myself in those soulful, heartfelt songs, weaving my saxophone phrases around his vocal lines. The band was a joy to play with and seemed to create a sense of spaciousness in the music and it had been a thrill to step out with the occasional solo. Now, however, with the excitement and adrenaline draining from my system I'm finding, with no small sense of rising alarm, that it's becoming increasingly hard to breathe. I pull over at a lay-by to rest a moment, exhausted with the effort of getting oxygen into my lungs. My head hangs forward and clutching onto the steering wheel I inwardly curse those kids.

Some three weeks before I'd been messing around horse-playing with Nuala and Layla and couple of their little friends, taking it in turns to let them ride on my back as I walked 'on all fours' around the room. I could never resist being the 'fun dad'. It developed into a free-for-all, the girls deciding I was a great interactive trampoline. One of the girls leapt on me whilst I was on my back bringing her pointy knees directly onto my ribcage. I felt something snap internally. At the time nothing hurt so I thought no more of it. A few days later I'd just completed a run of Alexander lessons and on leaving my workplace found that I could barely walk more than fifty yards without a severe pain in my chest. Apparently, I'd torn the cartilage on two or three of my ribs where they join to the sternum. I was advised to live quietly for a couple of weeks and avoid too much exertion.

When the phone call had come to do the gig with John, I'd optimistically assumed I'd be fit to play. I hadn't reckoned that blowing into a saxophone in front of a packed audience would open up old wounds. I did make it home in the end but a few moments horseplay had literally taken the wind out my sails.

It was Brian Young, who had recorded much of the Cado Belle material in the seventies at his Ca-Va studios who gave me the call. This was in the spring of 1984. I had to pinch myself. John Martyn was recording an album at his studios and Brian had suggested to John that I could provide some sax on some of the tracks.

John was in good form: affable, witty, open and seemingly positive about my musical contribution. He had been over in The Bahaas, at Compass Point Studios in

Nassau, laying down the tracks for 'Sapphire' and had returned to Scotland to finish them off. I played on three tunes. One of them, 'Climbing the Walls', I took home with me and worked on an arrangement. I came up with some Arabic-style lines which I overdubbed with alto and soprano saxophones. I thought they sounded neat and funky and John seemed to approve.

I'd passed the audition, as it were, and over the next three years I played on several of John's albums. John had at the time evolved far away from his folksy, finger-picking-guitar-style roots. He had, years before, succumbed to the allure of the electric guitar and in the seventies had pioneered a style based on the hypnotic cross-rhythm grooves offered up by the Echoplex machine, a device which allows the musician, through the use of echoes and delays, to build up rhythmic layers of sound. In the eighties, still searching for ways to expand the range of colour in his music he was now committed to the idea of fronting a band: drums, fretless bass, percussion, keyboards, and saxophone. Personally speaking, I prefer his earlier work. Back then, especially when underpinned by Danny Thompsons's bass, John's blurred and slurred vocals sound more vulnerable and passionate, more born of the troubles of first-hand experience than what we hear in his later work. But who was I to grumble? Here was I getting the chance to work with a truly unique artist.

After watching a nature programme on television about the astonishing and colourful displays produced by male birds-of-paradise to attract a mate, a friend once suggested that men in bands when performing on a stage, essentially have the same end in mind as those birds-of-paradise. It's an interesting proposition. Performing is very much a display and performers thrive on attention. Of course, whilst there have always been performers who love the attention they receive from the opposite sex, ultimately there have to be many reasons that bring people together to play music to an audience. For me, in my teens, music was the only thing I felt I had some ability with. I loved the status and identity of 'being in a band'. It became a way of covering up my shyness and lack of confidence. In my twenties it had become a way of life that was bordering on an addiction.

By the summer of 84, apart from the occasional frisson of playing with John Martyn I had now managed a year or so without involvement with a band. I was focussed on my new role of Alexander teacher and kept a busy schedule seeing up to forty clients a week. However, I began to sense that there was gap in my life. I began to crave a musical project to be engaged with, and the excitement of going out to play of an evening.

Ronnie, having split up with his girlfriend Christine was back in Glasgow and putting his energies into a new band which he named 'Festiva'. He invited me to join him. He recruited some of the best players around; rising star of jazz piano, Dave Newton; Patrick Bettison, a gifted young fretless bass player, fresh off the plane from Australia; Bobby Wishart, a Glaswegian jazz legend on sax and flute. Ronnie, still in love with the music of Brazil wrote ambitious tunes and arrangements developing what we'd done back in Devon with The Flying Dragons. This was big boys' music and in the company of such fluent improvisers who could confidently and creatively find their way through some serious chord sequences I often felt out of my depth. The band was short-lived, Dave and Patrick unable to resist the potential opportunities to open up their careers by moving to London, but on the few gigs we did play we gave our Glaswegian audiences a sophisticated and colourful performance the likes of which had never been heard in the city before.

It was Ronnie who introduced me to the Jacobsen sisters, Elin and Signe Jacobsdottir. They were at the time, as I recall, just eighteen and sixteen respectively but had a maturity and confidence beyond their years. Their father was Icelandic and they had been raised in what must have been a very cultured and creative household in Milngavie, on the outskirts of Glasgow. Like Ronnie, they were well into Brazilian music and both sang and played percussion. They showed up in my flat one day, all smiles and bright red lipstick and we sat on the living room floor discussing the possibility of playing some music together. How could I possibly resist forming a band with these two gorgeous and intelligent young women? We recruited a bass player from Edinburgh and an acoustic guitarist, John Gilmour.

John, who for some reason unknown to me had earned the nickname 'Fred Lawnmower', was a graduate from Glasgow School of Art. He was steeped in acoustic guitar style of Brazilian music and had a good understanding of the repertoire. The world of musicians is a small one but I was surprised to learn that John had, in a previous incarnation lived in Ireland where had played for a while with Errol in Stagalee. His girlfriend, Janice joined Signe and Elin on vocals, taking the lead in some songs and sharing harmonies in others.

John suggested we call the band 'Papo Furado.' Playing the Brazilian repertoire felt in some ways like a coming home for me. Since the Bossa Nova fashion had taken root in the sixties Brazilian music had become the 'easy listening' soundtrack of choice for public spaces, airports, lifts etc. I had rejected it as the old school music of a previous generation, far too smooth and comfortable for its own good. Now I was re-evaluating it and loving the chance to weave some flute lines over the rich harmonic progressions and subtle rhythm patterns, and I was learning new tunes by the likes of Reuben Blades and Antonio Carlos Jobim. Many of the musicians I admired had absorbed the Brazilian sound into their writing. An album I had endlessly listened to back in the seventies was 'Brazilian Love Affair' by jazz keyboardist, George Duke, a gorgeous mix of funk blended with all the best elements of Brazilian lyricism. Papo Furado was my chance to explore that rich landscape.

Another album with Mr Martyn came along. This was 'Piece by Piece', again recorded at Ca-Va Studios. John was living in a cottage in a remote village near Biggar at the time and it suited him to come up to Glasgow to record. He was still wedded to the idea of creating a bigger sound to flesh out his songs. Keyboards were very happening at the time and John had a new keyboardist, Foster Paterson who could ably produce a 'chorused' Rhodes piano sound with one hand simultaneously with a synthesised Japanese 'koto' sound on the other. Following on the album we did a six-date tour of the UK. We finished in a London theatre, supposedly the climax of the tour when music journalists would hopefully come up with positive reviews of John's latest incarnation. I remember John in the dressing room before the gig making noises that perhaps Phil Collins would show up and do a guest spot on drums. The ex-Genesis drummer and singer had sung backing vocals and drummed on one of John's previous albums, 'Grace and Danger' on the track 'Sweet Little Mystery'. It wasn't an unreasonable wish but Phil never showed up. Perhaps his solo career was too much on the ascendent at the time.

One thing that surprised me about John on the tour was his gift for mimicking accents. When chatting to fans in the dressing room in Newcastle he became a 'Geordie'; when in London, a Cockney geezer. I suppose some locals might have thought he was taking the Mick but it does say something about his prodigiously musical ear. Back at the hotel there would be rounds of drinks and joints passed. John could be quite amusing. He told us of a time years ago when he was really stoned and had decided to iron his shirt. He had recalled as a boy seeing his mother spit on the iron to see if it was hot enough. Lifting up the iron in his stoned state, instead of spitting on it he had licked it. Ouch!

Playing with John at this time took me to the Montreux Jazz Festival in Switzerland. In 1987 this was a major platform for jazz in Europe and attracted many top-flight American musicians. There was an artists' bar where musicians could hang out before and after performances. At the side of the bar was a small stage equipped with instruments and sound gear, an invitation for musicians to informally jam. Not being much of a party-animal I retired to my hotel room around 1pm and missed all the fun. I was told the next morning that around 3am, John's rhythm section, Alan and Aran had taken to the stage and had started up a groove. A series of jazz luminaries joined them in turn, the likes of Herbie Hancock, Stanley Clarke and George Benson. The music was flowing nicely with musicians enjoying the chance to play and throw ideas around. John was determined to join in on electric guitar. Unfortunately, he was by this time well hammered and spent an embarrassing ten minutes or so noisily tuning his guitar at the side of the stage with the jazz legends looking on and thinking, 'who is this guy?'

The following year a short tour of Israel with John was offered to me. Once again, the other band members were Foster on keyboards, Alan on bass and Aran on drums. Partners were invited to come along and I encouraged Anna to come. Cracks in my marriage were beginning to appear and I optimistically thought the trip might help to bridge the growing divide between us. As a child Anna had lived in Israel with her family for a while and I thought she'd enjoyed seeing the country again. John was still with Island Records at the time and they treated us to a little bit of pop-star luxury, three days in a five-star hotel with rooftop swimming pool on Tel Aviv's seafront. The itinerary was none too packed, just two concerts, giving time to visit the old walled city in Jerusalem and the Palestinian town of Jaffa, a few miles south of Tel Aviv.

The first gig was a bit of a non-event, playing to a largely under-whelmed small audience in a Tel Aviv nightclub. The other gig for me was somewhat surreal. This was an outdoor music festival supporting none other than the band, Jethro Tull. Compared to the stoned and mildly intoxicated atmosphere generated amongst fans at British music festivals the behaviour of the young Israeli audience was akin to something you might expect at an evangelical

Christian rally. They stood in quiet rows respectfully listening to the music and offering polite applause at the end of each tune. John was notorious for his drug-and-alcohol-embracing lifestyle. He was particularly something of a champion of marijuana and the freedom it supposedly represented. This reputation would sometimes be celebrated half way through his set when one of his roadies would ceremoniously come onto stage proffering John a freshly-rolled joint on a plump velvet cushion. As John inhaled deeply on the joint this theatrical act would normally elicit counter-cultural cheers from like-minded stoners in the audience. Not on this occasion: the velvet cushion and its prize were met with disinterested bemusement from the Israelis.

Watching Ian Anderson nearly twenty years after I had first seen him on Top of the Pops, still performing his stock-in-trade, one legged, eyeball-bulging antics was nothing short of bizarre. Back in the UK, Jethro Tull was a phenomenon associated with a musical fashion from long ago. The music scene there had watched punk, glam rock, and disco all take their turn in the spotlight over the past years. It was a surprise for me to learn that bands like Jethro Tull were still making a good living, touring around the world as they rode on the coat tails of their earlier success in the UK charts. Behind the unkempt, frizzy-haired facade Ian Anderson was a shrewd businessman. He had created a marketable music brand with longevity and had even bought himself an estate on the Isle of Skye with the profits. As a band leader I'm told he was exacting and disciplinarian and on that night in Tel Aviv he produced a very carefully crafted and entertaining set which went down well with the Israeli crowd.

After the festival concert, the Israeli guy who was looking after us, (his name now escapes me after all these years), took us to visit a friend of his. We drove to the northern outskirts of Tel Aviv and came to an industrial area, a kind of no-man's-land. Next to a huge gasometer, we turned down a dirt track and parked up next to a traditional Palestinian dwelling. A middle-aged man in a headscarf and robe gave us a warm welcome and invited us to join him in his garden. We sat on cushioned seats under an awning, candles flickering on a table and, serenaded by the night music of cicadas in the nearby bushes, our new friend's two wives brought us drinks and delicacies. As we sat under the stars in the gentle warmth of the Mediterranean air it felt like another world, far removed from the corporate superficiality of the hotel we'd been staying. Our host told us how he had built his home from scratch on a strip of industrial land where no Israeli would want to live. Marginalised by the Israeli state he had still managed to carve out himself a piece of paradise in this 'wasteland'.

Next morning, we gathered in the hotel lobby, waiting for our tour bus to take us to the airport. The bus arrived and we climbed on board with our belongings. John and his partner, Annie, still hadn't shown up. When they did eventually emerge from the hotel you could cut the atmosphere with a knife. John was dishevelled and obviously very hung-over. Annie allowed her long brown hair to tumble over her face but still didn't manage to disguise a nasty bruise around one of her eyes. In fact, they both looked like they had been scrapping. Annie looked pale and distraught, humiliated to be seen like this in front of the band members and crew, a victim of John's dark side. The tranquillity of our visit to the Palestinian dwelling must have evaporated in an alcohol-fuelled argument behind the closed door of their hotel bedroom. For all John championed the 'peace and love' associated with marijuana he was equally wedded to the irrational and destructive behaviour brought about by the 'demon alcohol'.

Back home I received an invitation. An old girlfriend, Anne Docherty, was getting married and kindly invited me along. 'Oh, and by the way', she had said, 'There might be a special guest'.

Anne had left Glasgow years before to train as a fashion designer in Newcastle. I'd lost touch but was now made aware that she was official 'dressmaker' to Tina Turner.

There weren't many guests at the wedding, perhaps around twenty-five. We sat in the round, enjoying the food and drink luxuries served up by the waitresses. There she was, just two places away from me. It was hard not to stare and I had to make do with furtive sidelong glances. Tina's beauty was astonishing. Somebody had told me she was 'one quarter Cherokee'. Perhaps this was what gave her skin such a lustrous golden hue and allowed her well-defined cheekbones to give her the look of a tribal princess. Under the luxuriant curls she exuded health and an astonishing vibrancy, like she was existing on a plane above us lesser mortals.

After the meal it wasn't long before the music started. A guest stood up and sang a traditional Scots song, possibly by Robert Burns. Anne had invited Maggie from Cado Belle to sing a song and had asked me to accompany her. She had particularly wanted Paul McCartney's 'Here, There, and

Everywhere'. I had brought along my Spanish guitar, recently purchased from a charity shop. Maggie and I had briefly rehearsed up the song the day before and we gave a passable rendition.

At this point, Tina approached. A few glasses of wine had by this point released the performer in her. She came and stood directly behind me and placed her hands on my shoulders as she addressed the wedding guests, exuding the energy of a pressure cooker needing to let off steam. Her hands massaged my shoulders as she spoke. This was surprising and I have to say, perfectly pleasant, but not quite as surreal as what happened next. One of her hands moved down my shirt and I was suddenly aware that she was casually caressing one of my nipples with her fingertips. Some quick-witted person took a photograph capturing this moment. In this photo I look blissed out, like someone in receipt of exquisite pleasure. I distinctly remember my nipple tingling in response to Tina's attentive finger-work. It was all very strange.

Without conferring with me she announced that she wanted to sing a tune that meant a lot to her when she was having problems with her 60's husband, Ike. This was 'Help' by The Beatles: a strange choice of song for Anne and her new husband's wedding day perhaps? Blimey, and not the easiest of chord sequences, I thought. The tune felt like it should be in the key of D major. I strummed a D chord. To my dismay Tina pitched in on the wrong starting note. Things were getting stranger. I had to stop and sing Tina the first note to get her into the right pitch. It briefly flashed through my mind that I was now in the role of tutoring a global megastar. We stumbled on into the song, Tina all passion and with me now struggling to find the right chord sequence. Tina's animated performance covered up all my guitar fumbles and by the end of the song all present were beaming smiles back at Tina, basking for those precious moments in her charismatic radiance, and perhaps not quite believing what they had just witnessed.

In the last four years of the 1980s the Pat Metheny band were touring 300 days each year. Goodness knows how they sustained meaningful relationships with their partners. However, that statistic does give a certain perspective to my comparatively limited music-making activities.

My ongoing pursuit of music could be seen in many ways. Was it a human version of the bird-of-paradise display to attract the opposite sex? Was it an earnest desire to develop my musical skills? Did I hope that music might one day take me into a hitherto unknown spiritual experience? Maybe the simplest and most down-to-earth explanation was that it was an interesting way to make money. Whatever the reason, the pursuit of music was causing big problems in my marriage to Anna. She increasingly thought I'd lost interest in her and we were going down different paths. By the end of 1988 she was signalling very clearly that she wanted out of our marriage.

A friend, Callum, came to visit. After staying with us for a couple of days and witnessing at first hand the general chaos in our household he diagnosed our marriage as suffering from a 'polarisation of interests'. This was a gentle understatement. I had by this time got involved with a spiritual group called 'The Keepers of the Flame' which certainly was poles away from Anna's current lifestyle.

One of the paths to enlightenment in the Tibetan Buddhist tradition is a daily discipline of chanting sacred words. This supposedly creates clarity and raises the vibrational level of the participant. One notable musician who regularly chants is Tina Turner who, in her later years has channelled her vocal energies into this discipline, perhaps leaving behind the past anguish expressed in songs such as 'What's Love Gotta Do with It?' for the calm solace brought on by aligning herself to a higher vibration. Herbie Hancock, the much-admired jazz pianist, is a proponent of chanting, having been steeped in the tradition for years. The 'Keepers of the Flame' also practiced chanting, calling the practice 'offering decrees'. Their belief was that it is possible through regularly 'decreeing' to align your vibration to those spiritual masters who exist on a higher plane. Through this practice one could reduce the burden of karma which holds us back from spiritual progress.

The 'Keepers' were a world-wide organisation with their base in the Rocky Mountains in Montana, USA. Our Glasgow group was very small, around half a dozen. We would meet regularly to offer decrees and support each other on our 'journeys'. Two members of the group were musicians; Christine Nelson, a violinist who played with one of the national orchestras and William Jackson, a traditional folk musician, specializing in the Celtic harp. When they turned up at our home in Lacrosse Terrace for one of our other-worldly chanting sessions in front of my little altar in the spare room, it soon became apparent that Anna and I were drifting in very different directions.

Life at Lacrosse Terrace stumbled on for a few more months. Anna began to make noises about moving down south to Bristol. I was frustrated and miserable but remained determined to do everything I could to keep our crumbling marriage going. In the spring of 1989, I moved to Bristol with her and the girls.

# 13 New City, New Beginnings

*'People say it takes a long time to become a jazz fan. For me, it took about five seconds.'*

*Pat Metheny*

Those first few months in Shirehampton, a village on the outskirts of Bristol were strange times. We had sold the flat in Lacrosse Terrace and had a little bit of money to get by. By this time, Anna now had a new partner and a new baby named Kenneth.

Taking the cue from Cathy Kiddel all those years before, we decided Nuala and Layla were to be home educated. They had briefly been attending a Steiner school in Glasgow so were already out of mainstream education. As newcomers to the area, we were below the radar of the local education authority so were for the time being free to do 'our own thing'

I poured all my attention into Nuala and Layla. Shirehampton, in contrast to Glasgow seemed very leafy and green and as the weather warmed up, I would take the girls for long nature walks to the River Avon or Blaise Castle estate. They were encouraged to draw and paint and back home we'd make up all kinds of plays. We became members of a home education group, known as Seed Circle, an eclectic group populated by free-thinking lefties and dedicated alternative educators. This provided some kind of social network for Nuala and Layla. Ultimately, however, entertaining the children's needs outside the support of an institution like a school was proving to be hard work.

One day I got a call from Ali Burrows. Ali was an Alexander teacher with whom I had trained in Totnes. She was herself now running an Alexander Teacher training school and wondered if I'd like to come in and do some work there. My small pot of money was running out so I jumped at the chance.

Serendipity is a wonderful thing. The school was a vibrant place full of interesting people. But there was a young woman there whom I found particularly interesting. This was Julia. I thought she was gorgeous. When working with Alexander Technique we place hands on people to increase their sensory awareness and to guide their movement in everyday activities: sitting, standing, bending etc. When teaching a group, it is only fair and professional to share out your attention in an even-handed way. This became difficult as I began to find myself taking every opportunity to work with Julia.

Julia and I had our first date seeing Kevin Costner's epic production 'Dances with Wolves' at the cinema in Clifton. Not being much of a fashionista, I turned up in a pair of synthetic blue shell trousers, with an elasticated waistline. Julia appeared slightly surprised as I came off the bus, as I seemed to resemble an extra from a children's TV programme. Somehow, Julia looked past my questionable outfit choice and we soon became an item.

Julia was fantastic. She was all patience with me as I gradually allowed myself to adapt to being in a new relationship. As for her, becoming a 'step-mum' was no easy task given the huge potential for resentment coming from children who, more than anything, want to preserve the status quo.

I was still finding time to play music. Dave Goodier, the bass player from 'the 'Flying Dragons' had settled in Bristol and was playing with a band called 'Contos Sul'. Dave suggested to the band leader Henry Shaftoe that he should invite me on board. Contos Sul were a large outfit with a brass section and vocalist, Teri Bramah. Henry played the vibraphone and wrote most of the Latin-tinged tunes. I played regularly with them for a year or so before Henry got fed up with all the organisation it takes to run a nine-piece band. Henry had a smaller, different unit in mind, and invited me to join him. This band became known as 'Tierra Colorada.'

In very obvious ways Tierra Colorada recalled to me my eighties band back in Glasgow, Papa Furado: both bands played Latin music and were fronted by three attractive women. In Tierra Colorada we had the two singers, Heo Legoretta from Mexico and Eugenia Ledesma from Argentina, alongside Lisa Cherian from Australia on congas. Adding to our pan-global array we had 'Coco' Kanyinde, a diminutive master drummer from Zaire on congas and Ricardo from Mexico on violin and charanga. We Anglo-Saxons were in the minority. I played mainly flute and a small amount of sax and Henry temporarily forsook his beloved vibraphone and moved onto drum-kit.

With the exotic provenance of our players Tierra was able to deliver a more authentic blend of Latin music. Heo and Eugenia knew the repertoire and guided us into playing songs in the Colombian 'cumbia' style and Cuban 'son-montuno' tradition. One of our finest moments happened one time when we were playing in central Bristol and were joined on stage by one of the top exponents of 'cumbia', Toto la Mompasina. She was at the time quite an elderly lady but her energy and vitality nearly blew us relative youngsters off the stage with her big voice and stage presence.

Another top gig with this band was aboard The Waverley steamship. This for me was a trip down memory lane. The Waverley is an old-fashioned paddle steamer that back in the day used to carry passengers to the islands of Arran and Bute in the Firth of Clyde. As a small boy I could remember during a trip to Arran going down below deck and being entranced by the sights, sounds and smells of the steam engine, a mesmerising complex of brass pipes and pistons that, like some gigantic metal-plated leviathan propelled the ship through the waves. Tierra Colorada had been booked to play on the Waverley on a journey from Ilfracombe in North Devon to Clevedon. Once on board I headed straight down to the engine room. To once again witness the hissing and pumping of the inner workings of the ship transported me back a few decades.

The band set up above deck and began to play. It was late afternoon on a fine and warm summer's day. I was initially disappointed that very few people emerged from the comfort of the lounge down below to hear us play. However, the disappointment was replaced by something which felt for me like a kind of peak experience. As we played, our music began to take on a kind of luminous beauty as the undulating hypnotic patterns of the 'montuno' reverberated from the ship's deck across the water towards the passing cliffs. The weather-worn contours of the North Devon coastline etched by the low evening light became our very own video accompaniment to our music as the old steamer ploughed its way along.

In September 1993, Julia and I got married. We had a ceremony in Hereford, followed by a big party in the evening. I had organised Tierra Colorada to come and play, their style of music being good to dance to. It is with a slight sense of embarrassment that I have to record that I couldn't resist the urge to play a couple of tunes with them. The fact that I couldn't devote the whole of this, my wedding day, to Julia is more evidence perhaps of my possibly incurable addiction to playing music, or to put it less kindly, my addiction to showing off.

Julia and I bought our first house together in Redland, Bristol. Our first daughter, Ailsa, arrived the following July. Her younger sister, Merryn, arrived in January, 1997. I was now proud dad to four daughters. How lucky was I.

Julia had finished her training as an Alexander teacher and together we kitted out our front room in Lansdown Road for teaching and began to build up a a shared private practice. My work at the Alexander Teacher training course also put money in the family coffers. With two young children to care for I tried to keep some kind of check on my musical activities not wanting to push my luck by taking on too many engagements. Julia continued to work as an artist alongside her Alexander teaching. We shared our parental and domestic duties and still had some time left over to indulge in our different passions.

One evening, driving back after a Tierra Colorada gig, the restless Henry came up with yet another idea for a band. He was keen to get back to writing and performing his own stuff and proposed that in a new band he and I could share a platform for our own compositions. This was the spark that ignited a new project which we called 'Sensorium'. We invited Duncan Kingston on bass and Ben Williams on keyboards to join us. I was also keen to have the talented and individual guitarist, Paul Bradley on board. The musical direction took a definite swing away from the Latin style of Tierra and Contos, with Sensorium attempting a marriage of Scots/Irish folk elements with jazz and funk.

I was very fired up with the new project and new tunes were soon emerging from both Henry and me. We rehearsed weekly at Ben's house for several months, building up the band's sound and a set of tunes we could get out and perform. I was very much under the spell of Jan Garbarek and tried to squeeze as much full-toned sonority out of my old 1930s Selmer saxophone. I'd been a fan of his since hearing him play with Keith Jarrett on their album, 'Arbour Zena' at Cromlix Estate back in the late seventies. Since those days Jan, as well as evolving a unique and distinctive palette of timbres on his instruments had pioneered a Euro-centric writing style which, whilst it incorporated many elements from music around the world, often evoked in the listener the vastness of mountain landscapes in northern Norway.

Sensorium did our first tentative gigs locally in Bristol. After hearing us perform, a friend at the time described the band's style as a Scottish-sounding version of Jan Garbarek's music. Suitably flattered we felt sufficiently encouraged to take the band into the studio and make an album. Bob's studio at The Bunker was the obvious choice. I had recorded there many times as a session musician. Besides, Bob was a friend and would give us 'mate's rates'. We squeezed ourselves into his recording room and put down about ten of Henry's and my tunes over a period of a few days.

There are some things in life you do which you're not proud of.

After listening to the recordings at home I decided I didn't like the approach of Ben's piano playing on some of the tracks. The sharp focus of the recording process had made me overly precious about how I wanted the music to sound. I was now faced with a choice; should I accept Ben's contribution as part of the group sound or should I go into Bob's and overdub the piano parts in the way I wanted it to sound? Given that choice nowadays I would like to think I would accept Ben's interpretation of the music. To wipe out all the hard graft, time and dedication of someone's input is morally indefensible. At the time however I was headstrong and ploughed ahead with replacing many of Ben's parts, in the astonishingly naive hope that Ben wouldn't mind. What was I thinking?! When he got to hear about it, Ben was, quite fittingly, incandescent with rage. My actions prompted a long and angry resignation letter. I lost a good friend and musical collaborator. I hope I have gained at least a modicum of wisdom from the experience.

Duncan, our bass player had been doing some gigs with a gifted young keyboard player, John Paul Gard and asked him to come and meet me. John came in to my living room all mischief and good humour and flicking back his shoulder length curls sat down and at the piano in my living room and played, as an unofficial audition piece, some of the changes from Coltrane's 'Giant Steps'. I was impressed. This boy could play much better than I could. I talked about the sound I was hoping to steer Sensorium towards and put a track on the CD player. This was 'His Eyes Were Suns' a pretty far-out composition of Jan Garbarek's built around a 'yoik', a kind of yodelling refrain peculiar to the Sami reindeer herders of northern Scandinavia. The pentatonic melody is underpinned with arresting keyboard polychords whilst Garbarek treats us to impossibly high yearning notes in the altissimo register, the whole perhaps evoking pictures of reindeer herds crossing vast snow-bound landscapes. Being a strange and exotic piece, it must have been quite an earful for John and goodness knows what was going through his mind at the time. I don't think 'His Eyes Were Suns' was quite John's 'bag' but he tactfully declared it was a beautiful piece of music and agreed to come along to the next Sensorium rehearsal.

Having someone of John's musicality and experience gave Sensorium a shot in the arm. John had good ears and quickly found his way into the set. Following on from our first release, 'Celtic Fields', we recorded a second album. 'A Fine Line', recorded live at the Queen Elizabeth Theatre in Bristol. Given that they were released independently and we had no distribution deal, the albums sold quite well. Audiences seemed to like our melodic blend of jazz and Celtic themes and would often purchase copies of the CDs at gigs.

I had at that point never considered myself much of a jazz improviser. I had in my younger years transcribed and learned a few Charlie Parker solos trying to acquaint myself with the great man's approach but I had never gone through the process of learning the jazz standards of the 'Great American Songbook', something that most competent jazz players have worked through as a basis for improvising. Although improvisation was an important element in Sensorium the harmonic changes were simple and easy to interpret.

One day I was given a call to do a 'proper' jazz gig as part of a trio in a café diner in the centre of Bristol. This establishment was known as 'Tantric Jazz' and was one of the few venues in town putting on live music on a regular basis. The double bass player Mike Wilsh was the MD and organised some of the regular sessions. Now in my forties, I was at last being given the chance to tackle the classic jazz repertoire. With just a double bass and piano there was no hiding. The alto sax had to carry the tune and ride the harmonic changes. It was initially quite a 'roast', having to sight-read the 'head' and then produce an improvised solo over the songs harmonic structure. Mike and the regular piano player, Andy Christie, who could effortlessly improvise on all the old tunes, were very supportive and let me feel my way into the role. It was gratifying to be asked back after that first gig and playing with Mike and Andy became a weekly fixture for quite some time. This was not 'cutting-edge' jazz but I loved the challenge and learned a lot.

From the mid-nineties I had settled into a work routine of teaching a couple of mornings at the Alexander Training

School, seeing several private pupils per week and playing music on some evenings. On a couple of mornings, I would take Ailsa and Merryn down to the local playgroup. It was here I had befriended Paul Bradley. Paul had a maverick reputation as a musician who had played in various innovative local bands. As we trundled our separate offspring in their buggies around the streets of Redland, I eventually managed to persuade Paul to become a member of Sensorium. Around this time, we also began to perform duo gigs together.

Paul was one of the first musicians to acquire in the early nineties a piece of kit known as the 'Jam-Man'. This essentially was a 'loop-recorder' which allowed the musician in a 'live' situation to record a phrase or chord sequence and then record multiple layers on top. Paul became a total craftsman with this device and deservedly earned the nickname 'Loopmeister' from his friends. Paul was an imaginative composer on the guitar and could elicit a whole rich vocabulary of sounds and styles. He also had a beautiful voice with something like a five-octave range. With such an artillery of musical possibilities at his fingertips he had begun to perform some entertaining solo gigs where everything he played was extemporised; guitar phrases, vocals and even lyrics were freshly minted on the spot.

Ganam, the Iraqi-born manager of Tantric Jazz was open to trying new sounds and took up my suggestion of Paul and I doing a weekly gig there. As well as my alto and soprano saxophones I brought a large Chilean 'bomba' drum to accompany Paul. With Paul's looped 'beatbox' vocals and my drumming on the goatskin drum we could build some nice grooves upon which all manner of musical journeys could be undertaken. Paul's imagination was fearless and seldom short on ideas. In one moment, he could be laying down a yearning chord sequence which I would try to compliment with plaintive Garbarek-esque lines on the soprano; the next moment Paul would be channelling Jimi Hendrix over a soulful backbeat, his wild guitar phrases pinning astonished diners to the back of their seats. To perform without any pre-planned set was exciting and ambitious but between us we often conjured up, what sounded to me, like great music.

One evening at Tantric Jazz we were approached by a young Iraqi guy who introduced himself as 'R F'. He had been listening appreciatively to our set. 'R F' was heading back soon to his home country and wondered if we had a CD of our music to take back with him. Finding out that we had never recorded our musical experiments he pulled out his wallet, thrust a couple of hundred quid into Paul's hand and insisted we go into the studio.

Suitably encouraged by 'R F's gift we booked ourselves into Bob's and made some recordings. Again, the philosophy was to be completely unscripted, eschewing even the use of 'overdubs'. By now we were calling ourselves 'Spirit Readers' and Paul named the album 'Any Normal Psychic'. The cover of the album featured a photograph of Henry's, a blue tinged image of an ice-bound pond, the cracks on the icy surface reminding me of the wispy strands of ectoplasm associated with Victorian spiritual mediums. In the tradition of the 'Incredible String Band' we both played an array of instruments; saxophones, guitar, harmonica, melodica, drums and tin whistles, all taking their turn over Paul's loping electric guitar loops. Paul also improvised some lyrics in a couple of tunes and treated us at the beginning of one track to the full use of his five-octave vocal range in what sounded to my ears like an over-excited muezzin reciting his call to prayer. Again, like the Sensorium albums, we had no distribution or label to back us and simply sold copies of 'Any Normal Psychic' at our gigs.

Julia and I hankered after a move to the countryside. On days off we would make exploratory journeys to the small towns and villages within a thirty-mile radius of Bristol: Nailsworth, Stroud, The Mendips, Clevedon, Chepstow and Thornbury. It became a kind of obsessive game of trying to picture ourselves living the idyllic country dream, a theme which has been the basis of many TV series over the past twenty years. However, months went by and each location on our list just didn't seem right for us.

Julia's parents, lived on the outskirts of Monmouth just beyond our radius of exploration. As we visited them with our young children, we gradually warmed to the idea of moving closer to them. An increasing familiarity with the Black Mountains and the unspoiled landscape tempted us to eventually buy our house in Monmouthshire.

In April 2002, we moved to a small, sleepy hamlet outside Monmouth, turning the page to begin a whole new chapter.

# 14 New Musical Pathways

*'When you do something noble and beautiful and nobody notices,
don't be sad. For the sun every morning is a beautiful spectacle and yet
most of the audience still sleeps.'*

*John Lennon*

I can't quite believe our good fortune. The move from
city to countryside is everything we hoped for and more.
Our new home, a converted forge on the Rolls estate
outside Monmouth is brimful with character, old beams
support the ceiling, wooden shutters covering the windows
at night. Various pieces of ironwork protrude from the walls
inside, evidence of the house's industrial past; hooks to
tether horses as they were being shod, a selection of
blacksmith's tongs above the fireplace where the furnace
used to be. Outside, a small brook runs along the bottom of
the garden across which we have a panoramic view of our
neighbours' woodland. At the beginning of April, under the
alders and birches, there is a floral carpet of wood
anemonies and celandines, which a few weeks later gives
way to our very own display of bluebells. In our 'postage
stamp' of a garden in Bristol we would see an average of
about one bird over the course of a year, a situation brought

on by the high density of cats in the neighbourhood there. Here, in this corner of Monmouthshire, our ears are treated to the continuous calls of garden and woodland birds, occasionally under-scored by the hammer-drill percussion of woodpeckers seeking out insects under the bark of trees. The maniacal laughing calls of their cousins, the green woodpeckers, cackle to us from the nearby fields. A tawny owl visits us during our first week, breathtakingly large as he boldly perches on the fence outside our back window, his saucer eyes fascinated by the movement of Ailsa and Merryn's guinea pigs in their hutch.

When my Auntie Effie died back in the nineties her lovely old baby grand piano which she had purchased before the second world war was given to my niece, Susan. Susan was playing a lot at the time and the piano graced her living room in Glasgow for a number of years. One day I received a message from her mum, Fiona, that Susan would like me to have the piano. She was moving and the piano wouldn't fit into her new house Her bad luck became our good fortune as we now had a living room large enough to accommodate the instrument.

The piano arrived, complete with the bonus of decades-old coal dust from Effie's living room fire which had accumulated thickly in its interior. When I lifted the piano lid, I was transported by the sooty aroma back to my childhood in the 60s when my family would visit Auntie Effie in her tiny flat in North Kelvinside. There, after rounds of sandwiches and cake, we would be entertained by Effie and my father playing piano duets by the likes of Grieg and Muscovsky, duets which they had been playing together since the 1920s.

Thank you, Susan. It's been a joy and a privilege to have such a lovely old instrument to play on over the years since it arrived.

The move to Monmouth, an hour's drive from Bristol, necessitated a re-think regarding how I was earning a living. I maintained some teaching, one day per week at The Alexander training School. I also began to build up a private Alexander practice in the local natural health centre. However, these activities were not paying all the bills so I therefore applied for work as a peripatetic woodwind teacher with the local authority. This would entail me visiting several schools throughout the county. I was slightly surprised when I breezed through my interview for the job. Sure, I did have a music degree under my belt but under normal circumstances peripatetic teachers are expected to have done their respective music grades on the instruments they are teaching, at least up to grade eight level. I had no grades whatsoever on woodwinds. I did feel confident enough to be able to teach flute and saxophone but decided it would perhaps be tactful not to confide in my interviewer, Paul Hornsby, that teaching clarinet presented more of a problem for me. Not only could I not play the clarinet, I didn't even own an instrument. With my first lessons scheduled within days I quickly, and luckily, acquired a clarinet from a neighbour. It had been 'gathering dust under her daughter's bed for years'. I bought myself a tutor book and gave myself a crash course in clarinet playing. Thereafter it was just a case of keeping one step ahead of my clarinet pupils.

With Auntie Effie's Glaswegian instrument now beckoning to me every time I passed it, I began to play more piano. Our new house was very open-plan in design and the sound of the piano rang out in the living room, kitchen and upstairs into the bedrooms. As far as I was concerned it was a beautiful and reverberant acoustic. However, if Julia, Ailsa or Merryn should decide that they didn't particularly want to hear my piano tinkerings at a given time there was little escape other than by asking me, begging me even, to stop.

I began to form a plan. Perhaps if I could get a gig as a piano player in a hotel then I would get a chance to tinker to my heart's content. I put out some feelers and a few weeks later was given the chance to play in The Angel Hotel in Abergavenny. William Griffiths had recently taken over the running of this old Georgian coaching inn. At the time the hotel was a bit run down but William had big plans to raise its profile. Fortunately for me, having live piano music on Friday and Saturday evenings fitted nicely into William's vision of elegance and comfort for his new establishment.

For the first few weeks I sat in the bar. It featured a mixed clientele of diners who sat at the tables, and locals crowding around the bar with their cronies. William suggested I played for four hours with breaks. This, given my very limited repertoire of tunes was considerably more than I'd bargained for. I could only tease out a dozen or so tunes to last an hour or so. Repetition of my 'set' seemed a bit like cheating but was necessary for those first few weeks. My reading skills on single- line woodwind instruments like the saxophone were adequate but reading two staved piano music was a skill I'd largely lost back in my teens. Finding new repertoire to play by reading sheet music wasn't really a viable option.

Rather than feeling frustrated about my poor reading skills I decide to relish the opportunity to play everything by ear and to develop my improvising abilities. As long as I could recall a melody in my head, I loved the challenge of having a go at translating it onto the piano and finding the appropriate harmonic under structure. This involved guesswork and the occasional fumbled note but in time the sequencing of muscular memory would take over. Besides, playing in a hotel bar was the perfect place to develop these skills as no one was listening too intently. Eventually William suggested I moved into the restaurant. This was a more refined environment than the bar which by 10 pm was full of people alcoholically fuelled up for a sing-song. In the restaurant the piano music would waft around the tables hopefully creating an appreciable difference to the diners' experience.

My repertoire on the piano was, at worst, unfocused; at best, eclectic. I would play all sorts of cod arrangements of classical pieces, jazz standards, folk tunes and my own compositional ideas. I learned to 'walk the bass' and play through old blues tunes. Sometimes I'd delve into things I'd heard decades ago, even versions of tunes by the Incredible String Band, enjoying the journey through past phases of my life. From the vaults of my memory, I pulled out a Freddie King tune, 'The Stumble' which I'd heard forty years before during my first rock concert at the Electric Gardens in Glasgow. I was amazed I could still recall all the phrases in my head but after a few weeks of practice I was able to deliver a decent rendition.

Sometimes it could feel lonely playing for four hours on my own, so I'd focus myself on playing tunes written by or associated with friends and family, imagining that I was sending them the tune as it were, telepathically across the airwaves. At other times it felt like I was channelling the spirit of my father who, at the drop of a hat, would sit himself at a piano with any gathering of people and play a tune. On one level this could be seen as a desire to show off; on another, just a desire to express something beautiful or joyful and perhaps change the mood of someone who happens to be listening. At times I'd be so lost in the mood I was generating in the music that I'd temporarily lose connection with time and place. On one occasion I was so 'off' and into the music, eyes closed as I searched out the next phrase, that I got quite a shock to find William leaning over in my direction enquiring if I was quite alright.

One day I received a call from John Martyn's long-standing bass player, Alan Thomson. I hadn't heard from Alan in several years. John was playing at St David's Hall in Cardiff that evening and would I come and play some saxophone?

At the sound check it was good to be reunited with Alan and drummer, Aran Amun, who had both done the gigs in Israel with me back in the 80's. Foster Paterson had been replaced some years before by another keyboard ace, Spencer Cousins. Alan talked me through the tunes as John by now wasn't bothering himself with sound checks, preferring to relax before the gig at his hotel.

The concert was meant to start at 8:30 but by 8:40 there was still no sign of John. An audience of his devotees had already filled the auditorium. His fans would have known he was unpredictable; that was part of his charm, but they were getting restless. The thought briefly crossed my mind that John had blown out gigs in the distant past, by getting too hammered in the hotel beforehand to be able to perform. These days, I'd heard, he was a bit more professional. Suddenly there was a rumpus at the end the corridor which ran the length of the dressing rooms backstage. John had arrived. It was at least ten years since I'd last seen him and nothing could have quite prepared me for the change in his appearance. Coming along the corridor in a wheelchair pushed by a minder, along with his current partner, Theresa, was John, drunk and loud-mouthed and about several stones heavier that when I'd last seen him. He nevertheless seemed buoyant and suitably adrenalised for his gig. The minder stopped John's chair in front of a dressing room where a local drug dealer had laid out a line of cocaine for the great man. It became apparent that the wheelchair was too wide to get through the doorway. 'Where's ma leg?' John's voice sounded hoarse with frustration. The demand was both shocking and pitiful in equal measure. From somewhere on the back of the wheelchair a prosthetic limb was produced ready to attached onto John's amputated leg. (His leg had been amputated in 2004 when a massive 'baker's cist' in his knee joint had burst). In the end there was no need for the prosthetic limb as the dealer brought out the white powder on a plate. John lifted the plate to his nose and, with a well-practiced sideways flick of his head, sniffed the powder up his nostrils.

Suitably fired up for performance John was helped up the steps leading to the side of the stage. From here he would attempt to walk unassisted to the microphone at the front. Somebody brought him a walking stick, not your average pensioner's walking aid but a sturdy long staff, the kind that Moses would have had in a Hollywood epic. To complete his messianic image, he wore an Islamic 'jubba', a long robe which conveniently covered any missing body parts. The gathering of loyal disciples in the theatre erupted in applause as they saw this latest enrobed and corpulent version of their hero move stiffly to his chair, positioned centre stage.

Once ensconced in his high chair he delivered his usual barrage of off-the-cuff witticisms into the mic with all the charm and excitement of a schoolboy telling a new joke. His delivery was so fast and mumbled I couldn't make out what he was saying. The audience, however, seemed to appreciate his banter. Here was the anti-establishment, unpredictable legend they had paid good money to see, still able to get up there on stage and represent the Bohemian spirit of the sixties. Then it was into the music. John delivered a set of tunes selected from the large discography of twenty or so albums he had produced over the decades, his vocals all passion and nuance.

Playing in St David's Hall transported me back to what was perhaps one of the most exciting gigs of my life playing the pyramid stage at Glastonbury festival with John in 1986. Nothing had prepared me for the massive size of the audience when I had first stepped onto that hallowed space. To be on the receiving end of that huge wave of appreciation from the sea of humanity stretching out in front of you was both astonishing and empowering. I could understand how the experience could become addictive. Back then a slot in the set had to be allocated to John's most famous song, 'May you Never' the words of which the Glastonbury crowd worshipfully sang along with John. At St David's Hall this tradition continued. A roadie handed John his acoustic guitar, a symbol of his folk roots. He expertly picked at the de-tuned strings in that Davy Graham, 'claw-hammer' style he had perfected back in the sixties. The crowd, recognising the opening guitar phrases, erupted into a ripple of cheering. The words:

"May you never lay your head down without a hand to hold
May you never make your bed out in the cold'

rang out over the assembly of devotees, a blessing from their spiritual master.

Meanwhile, my Bristol band, Sensorium limped on. Now that I lived an hour's drive from the city the possibility of rehearsing up new material became more challenging. The other musicians, Duncan, John, Paul and Henry all had other music projects on the go and Sensorium only ventured out to play a few times a year. Promoting your own gigs takes up a lot of energy and time. A couple of memorable concerts come to mind; playing in a large candle-lit cavern at the Clearwell Caves was certainly a unique experience and The Savoy Theatre, where we managed to pull a crowd of a couple of hundred people, was also a band highlight.

One year, we found ourselves playing at the Pontypool Jazz Festival in South Wales. The festival took place in a Victorian public park. In the old bandstand near the marquee where we were scheduled to play, I noticed a lone figure playing the saxophone. Moving a bit closer I was surprised to recognise Nik Turner of Hawkwind fame. It must have been some thirty years since I shared a joint of Thai grass with him in that old vicarage, back in my Cado Belle days. Still very much a counter-cultural figure he had invited himself to the festival. As he blew his horn and kept a beat by tapping a tambourine at his feet, I got the sense that he was conducting a kind of protest against those 'establishment' figures who ran the festival who hadn't thought to invite him. He was going to show them where music was 'really at'; the consciousness raising revolution of the hippy era must go on. It is always interesting to see what happens to musicians who have achieved fame in their younger years. Do they give up music and take up another career? I got chatting to Nik. He seemed to be doing the odd gig here with collaborators from former bands but he told me that lately he had taken to busking in Cardiff town centre. 'Just play the Pink Panther and the money comes flying in' he advised with a chuckle.

After nearly twenty years Sensorium's swan-song finally arrived. In 2011, I decided to celebrate the band's long existence with a final short Scottish tour.

2011 happened to be the thirty years anniversary of the release of Gregory's Girl. Having witnessed the huge popularity of the film and how it had especially won a place in the hearts of many Scottish people I formed a plan. Although through the years I'd often wanted to distance myself from the film's music, considering it as being a bit shallow and old-fashioned, I was now more than happy to re-embrace it. I put together a selection of the some of the themes into a 'Gregory's Girl Suite' which I got Sensorium to rehearse. I contacted my old friend, Jim Wilkie, who had organised the Highlands and Islands tours back in the day with Cado Belle, and asked him if he could put together a short tour for Sensorium, riding on the coat tails of Gregory's Girl. Jim came up trumps and secured us some dates built around a slot at the Glasgow Jazz Festival. Ronnie joined us for a couple of the gigs, playing congas and percussion. In a bar off Glasgow's Bath Street, I experienced a bit of time travel as we played our tunes, Jim joining us for a few numbers, many key inhabitants of my former Glaswegian life back in the seventies and eighties milling around for a chat after we'd finished playing, amongst them Davy and Maggie from Cado Belle and Brian Young from Ca-Va recording studio, everyone looking just a wee bit older.

Meanwhile domestic life at The Forge continued happily. Ailsa and Merryn were thriving at the local school. We even had the luxury of a school bus picking them up from our road end in the mornings. At the weekend we enjoyed exploring local walks together and taking trips into the Black Mountains to climb Skirrid Fawr and the Sugar Loaf, bribing the girls with sweets if they would just climb another 100 yards.

The children were now at an age where we felt they could take on a musical instrument. Ailsa, two years older than Merryn began to play my clarinet. I had by this time got a reasonable grip of the instrument in order to be able to teach her. A couple of years later I took a slightly random decision: we'd get Merryn a violin and Ailsa would start on the cello; I'd cultivate my very own 'home grown' string section.

Sometimes life takes you full circle.

After leaving the choir and rejecting the church music tradition aged fifteen, deciding it was an embarrassing mismatch with my teenage aspirations, there had often been times when I looked back to the experience of being in a choir with a mixture of gratitude and nostalgia. One particular memory comes to mind.

I must have been 22 when, after going through a recent painful breakup with a girlfriend, I took the bus from Glasgow out to Eaglesham to visit my parents. It was when I was walking down the long road to their house that I was suddenly overwhelmed with a huge feeling of loss. The sobs came and by the time I reached their house I was in bits. The breakup with my girlfriend, which had weighed heavily in my mind had now made its way to my chest. However, what had actually triggered the sobbing was the Christmas carol 'In the Bleak Midwinter', Harold Darke's version, which, for some reason I had started to hear in my head. The carol which I'd sung years before as a choirboy was now a catalyst for emotions associated with the breakup, which, I can only guess, I'd been carrying around stored up in muscular memory.

It's a strange paradox but I have often found that the release of tears can lead to a sense of joy; after the tears I can sometimes experience something that could be described as bliss, an intense feeling of love of and appreciation for life. Such was my happy/sad state on arrival at my parents. They must have been very confused.

An increase in respect for my choral training began then. I can now see, from the perspective of my current great age of 66, that having my young ears immersed in choral music three of four times a week was the single most important aspect of my musical training.

Across the fields from where we live is a small church named after the seventh century Welsh saint, St Cadoc. Andrew Greenwood, a conductor and ex-director of the Welsh National Opera moved to a house next to the church and began to establish a choir there. In September, 2006 I got chatting to him and his wife Sara in the lane outside our house. It was probably when I mentioned that I composed music for my band that they proposed that I could write a carol for the choir to sing at the forthcoming Christmas service. The idea took hold. I found a suitable text in my father's old hymn books, waited for the moment when the melody revealed itself, then sat at the piano for hours, jotting down the harmonies and counterpoint in a manuscript book. This was a slow and laborious process for me but my exposure to choir training all those years before helped enormously in going about the task. One day in early December I took my first carol across the fields to show to Andrew. It was by no means a great work of art but I was thrilled to hear Andrew play it through at the piano and make encouraging noises.

That was the start of an annual pattern. In the autumn I would start to root around for a suitable text to set to music and would put a new carol together in time for the choir to rehearse it up before Christmas. I bought myself Sibelius music-writing software. This, coupled with the growing confidence I gained from 'learning on the job,' made the process of writing the carols quicker as the years went by. When it came to the performance, I would sing bass in the choir and it was always a slightly uneasy and surreal experience to hear your five-minute creation coming to life around you. I can scarcely mention my name in the same sentence as the great American composer, Aaron Copland, but I read somewhere that for him the special moments of his life were those times when he arrived at a concert hall to hear a piece that he'd been writing in seclusion for several months finally come to life in a first performance. At these carol concerts I could get perhaps the slightest flavour of how he felt.

I mentioned earlier that our house was a former forge on the Rolls estate. Over the years of living there I began to take an interest in the life of Charles Rolls of Rolls-Royce fame. We had a great early photograph of the blacksmiths standing in front of the forge back in the 1900's, proudly showing off an aircraft launcher that Charles had commissioned them to construct. In the early days of aviation, an aircraft launcher functioned like a huge catapult, propelling the aeroplane along a rail at great speed, giving it sufficient momentum to take off. It was after his flimsy aircraft had been launched by one of these contraptions that it tumbled from the sky at an air-show in Bournemouth in 1910, killing Charles at the young age of 32 as it struck the ground.

In late 2009, knowing that it was soon to be the 100th anniversary of Charles Rolls' death, an idea began to grow in me. It was when I was walking our dog Tilly along the path across the fields that leads to St Cadoc's, a path that in the late nineteenth century would have been used by Charles and his family to make their way to church on Sunday, that the notion of writing a musical based on his life really took hold.

# 15 Let the Circle be Unbroken

*'To achieve great things, two things are needed: a plan and not quite enough time.'*

*Leonard Bernstein*

My first job was to rid myself of my prejudice against musicals. I had long stubbornly held the view that actors suddenly bursting into song during a good story was silly and contrived. It didn't happen in real life so why should it on a stage or in a film? On the other hand, however, I had to confess that I enjoyed many of the songs when heard away from the context of the musical they were written for. I particularly began to re-evaluate the work of melodic genius, Richard Rogers.

Rogers wrote the music to some fifty musicals in his lifetime and many of his songs still have resonance today: Blue Moon, Oh what a Beautiful Morning, You'll Never Walk Alone, Younger than Springtime, not to mention the songs from 'The Sound of Music' which include 'My Favourite Things', a tune adopted and often played by the great tenor saxophonist, John Coltrane. I recalled a gig in Bristol back in the nineties when I heard my guitarist friend Paul Bradley doing a version of 'Oh What a Beautiful

Morning' in amongst a set of his own off-the-cuff, loop-based creations and found myself falling in love with the poignant innocence of its lyric and melody.

Over a couple of weeks, the first songs for my musical took hold in my imagination. There was an interesting story to be told and apart from adding in a fictional love interest, I considered, perhaps naively, that the different colourful events in Charles Rolls' short life were enough in themselves to form the basis of an entertaining musical.

As I ploughed my way into the project, I began to sense the enormity of what I was taking on. With my various jobs of teaching Alexander Technique and woodwinds, my weekly commitment at The Angel, alongside domestic and family responsibilities it was going to be a struggle to find the space for writing. By Christmas, I was becoming bogged down and ready to quit the whole idea of writing the musical when my daughter, Ailsa gave the project an injection of new enthusiasm.

I had noticed Ailsa's natural musical ability from a young age. I remember singing a song with her at bath time when she was only two years old and being surprised that she effortlessly kept in pitch with her little voice. Around the age of nine we got her a half-size cello. She progressed well with this and went through some music grade exams. She also had a go with my clarinet and together we developed a repertoire of tunes she could play 'by ear'. This came in handy when we had a family holiday in Tuscany.

Please, dear reader, when you read the next sentence, cast all thoughts from your mind that I was exploiting my daughter's talents for commercial gain. In the spirit of giving Ailsa 'valuable performing experience' we would go out into the streets of Barga and busk. I played a little hand-held, mouth-blown keyboard called a melodica to accompany her clarinet. We played a whole range of tunes, from folk songs to Beatles melodies. Our music was unobtrusive and resonated sweetly amongst the masonry of the old town. After an hour of playing, the twelve-year-old Ailsa was running out of puff and happy to stop. Then there was the fun of taking our 'hat' of money back home to see what we'd earned. On a couple of occasions, we had accumulated enough contributions from appreciative passers-by for us all to go out for a pizza.

At fifteen, Ailsa was excited about the idea of her dad writing a musical. I encouraged her to write a song for it and she came up with a promising melody which later became one of the main themes of the musical; 'If It were a Different World', a ballad shared between Charles and his childhood sweetheart, Lizzie. It was when Ailsa and I were putting this song together that I felt I'd turned a corner; there was now no going back.

So began an intense period of six months when I was obsessed with creating 'Charlie Rolls, the Musical'. Julia was incredibly tolerant given that I was still working my various jobs and every available moment of my spare time was taken up by the project. Perhaps she benefitted in a small way from my taking every opportunity to volunteer to walk the dog. I found that walking out in the fields would be a great time to compose and would often come back from these walks with a new verse written or a new fragment of melody ready to try at the piano. It was a self-imposed but monumental task to write lyrics and music for twelve songs, create the stage play and to root out singers, musicians and actors willing to take part but I have to say I totally loved every minute of the process.

The music evolved in an Edwardian style which felt appropriate to the period, a style my sixteen-year-old self would no doubt have found totally uncool. For one of the numbers, I even found myself writing in the tradition of what I later realised was a 'patter song', a fast-flowing tumble of words delivered at rapid speed by the singers, a style that I must have absorbed by osmosis when watching a school production of Gilbert and Sullivan's Mikado as a fourteen-year-old teenager.

My over-arching wish was to make the production an event that would draw the local community together. Rosie Whaley, a local headmistress with a fantastic contralto voice was perfect for the role of Charles' mother, Georgiana. Rosie welcomed the opportunity with open arms and helped to get some local funding for the project. We even did a prototype version of Charlie with pupils at her school, some of whom came on board for the main production. Andrew, our local celebrity conductor agreed to play for the performances and to be musical director and his wife Sara, agreed to play cello. As the play involved both aristocrats and lowly-paid estate workers I was keen to introduce folk music into the project. I was lucky to welcome local ceilidh musicians, fiddler Andrew Lane and his friend, ceilidh caller, Dick Wheelock into the production.

At the half-way stage, I was introduced to theatre director, Robin Tebbut. It was such a relief to me when he agreed to stage-manage the show. He also, like a Broadway script-editor, honed the first draft of my over-wordy stage-play into something much more fluid and enjoyable.

From the beginning I had in mind my friend and neighbour, Tony Vines, to play the lead role of Charlie. Not only did Tony have a great singing voice and a natural ability to act he also bore an uncanny resemblance to Charles Rolls. Tony also lent great support to the project, sorting out publicity, programmes and many other practical issues. His whole family gave up their summer to the musical; his partner, Clare, joined the cast, playing a posh aristocrat who enjoys balloon rides with Charlie and their young son, George, took on the important job of narrator.

Like magic, everything fell into place.

A half mile from our house is the Rolls mansion. It was here that Charles Rolls' father had his country estate. What had initially been a shooting lodge was developed over decades in the nineteenth century into a massive sprawling complex of buildings fit for an aristocratic family. John Rolls, Charles' father, was a baronet with a seat in the House of Lords. His family were London property owners who at one time were collecting 60,000 rents from tenants in Bermondsey and had also added to their wealth through prudent marriages.

In the mansion there is a room which was formerly the family lounge and it was here that Robin and I decided to stage the musical. To bring the story of Charles Rolls back to the house where he grew up was an opportunity not to be missed.

We did two shows on August 12th and 13th, 2010. We had a small band of musicians; Andrew Greenwood on piano, his wife Sara on cello, Andrew Lane on fiddle with myself on clarinet and soprano saxophone. We sold out on both nights, cramming as many people, around a hundred, on rows of seats into the former Rolls living room. After six months of preparation, it was a dream-like experience finally to be presenting the show. The actors did a great job, and the songs with their music-hall flavour hit the right note.

The audiences loved the show. We received standing ovations on both nights and I was on cloud nine, basking in the glow of positive comments and messages of appreciation. Some people suggested that the show should be taken to London's West End. I began to fantasise a bright future for the musical. This was, after all, a story of national significance. Its main protagonist, Charles Rolls, was a car-racing hero whose firm, Rolls-Royce, went on to build engines for planes like the Spitfire which saved us from Adolf Hitler. His pioneering endeavour coupled with the tragedy surrounding his untimely death surely was a story worth telling.

We put on Charlie Rolls again in November that year. This time I invited a theatre director who had worked with the stage production of Les Miserables in London, hoping he would see the musical's potential. I went to visit him a few days later to hear his response.

He didn't mince his words.

'Did I realise just how long it took to develop a musical fit for a London West End theatre? Did I realise that to bring Les Miserables to its current successful form had taken many years of development?' In his opinion, what I had created with Charlie Rolls was merely a sketch of Charles' life, hardly a musical.

He did throw me a morsel of compensation by telling me that he thought the band was 'quite good'.

I left, any dreams of having my name up in lights in London's West End crushed.

A family night out.

Julia, Ailsa, Merryn and I are heading to the lovely concert hall at St Georges, in Bristol. We have free tickets courtesy of our friend Phil, who happens to organise the Thursday night programme at the famous venue. For me, the act we are about to hear will be a trip down memory lane.

After some thirty years in relative obscurity, the sixties recordings of Vashti Bunyan have picked up a cult following with a new discerning and multi-generational audience. When one of her songs, 'It's Just Another Diamond Day' was used in a TV commercial her gentle evocation of a simple life, travelling through the UK in a horse-drawn wagon resonated both with a new generation of young listeners as well as people of her own age group, nostalgic for the dreamy possibilities of the hippy era. Driving over to Bristol I recalled the vulnerable and sensitive young woman I had met at Cromlix in the late seventies, too trammelled by the responsibilities of young motherhood to voice anything regarding her musical achievements.

She floats to the front of the stage and places her acoustic guitar on her lap. This is a woman with a new-found confidence and purpose. As far as I know she didn't do much performing and touring in her early career but now she seems comfortable with being in the limelight, talking to the audience in an assured way and, after so many years in the waiting, enjoying the opportunity to re-visit those songs penned so long ago. But her act is not all nostalgia. Spurred on by the revival of interest in her early work she is writing new songs and is accompanied by two musicians, a guitarist and folk fiddler who sensitively amplify her musical visions. Later, driving back to Monmouth, I regret I didn't call backstage to congratulate her, fearing that she might not remember me from all those years before.

Ailsa and Merryn are now away from home, allured like so many country-raised kids by London's glamour. Ailsa gets a chance to study music at Goldsmith's whereas Merryn gets a place the prestigious School of Oriental and African Studies where she studies anthropology and religion. They do, fortunately love coming home to the countryside for some fresh air. When at home, Merryn, with her interest in world culture regales us with the latest selection of musical discoveries she has made on the internet as she dances around the kitchen, pretending to wash the dishes. I dub her 'DJ Merryn'. These are joyful times and it's always sad to see them return to the The Big Smoke.

One evening I take Julia on a journey to make connections with a different phase of my life. This time memory lane leads us to a little village hall in the Forest of Dean. We are to hear Robin Williamson.

Robin has enjoyed a long solo career since the demise of the Incredible String Band. When I last saw him, some twenty years before, he had impressively evolved into a story teller, mainly accompanying himself on Celtic harp, displaying astonishing powers of recall as he recounted long, rambling but entertaining stories over the florid cadences of his harp, every inch the fully-fledged Celtic bard that was sometimes emergent in his String Band persona.

We step into the hall. Robin and his partner, Bina are already on stage. For once, we are not late arriving. Rather than following the tradition of being announced and coming onto the platform to start his performance, Robin is already seated on stage and for the ten minutes or so while we all gather, he chooses to carefully scrutinise his audience. It's somewhat disconcerting. Eventually, deciding that everyone who is coming has arrived, he introduces himself and his partner, Bina.

They give us a set of quirky songs, many of which seem to be culled from the repertoire of a rural community somewhere in the States, a place where Robin and Bina have lived for a while and absorbed the local music traditions. Robin now seems part ethnomusicologist, part entertainer. I have to remind myself that Robin is well into his seventies. While some of his contemporaries will be tucked up in blankets in rest homes, here he is, fully vital, still with that incredible ability to recall and perform songs, his fingers accurately plucking on harp and guitar. He is slim and wiry, having lost the more comfortable, corpulent shape of his middle years.

Whilst his voice is still strong and resonant, Bina's is frail and faltering. Back in days of the Incredible String Band, Robin and Mike, in a spirit of 'everyone is a musician', had their current girlfriends, Licorice and Rose join them in their music-making. Carrying on this tradition of inclusivity, Bina has long performed alongside Robin. I find her wavering, old lady's voice strangely moving.

At the end of the performance Robin is selling merchandise. Alongside his extensive back catalogue of CDs, he is offering prints of his artwork. Ever the renaissance man, he has been painting since ISB days: some are colourful bold portraits of Celtic saints, others are dreamy visual representations of lyrics from his songs over the past five decades, often woven through with Celtic knot work and the animated lettering typically used to illustrate the folk tales of the Brothers Grimm. The images are shot through with a spirituality reminiscent of the paintings of Cecil Collins.

Reaching the head of the queue and clutching a CD of 'The Merry Band', a group Robin worked with in California after the ISB split, I hand Robin some money and strike up a conversation. Knowing that he is likely to have endured a stream of compliments throughout a lifetime of performances I struggle to find something original to say and instead come out with bland praise. His musical ear picks up on my accent and he asks where I'm from. When I tell him of my Scottish origins, he becomes excited, telling me he was back up north, just recently. With a strange gleam in his eyes, he declares 'It was shining!' I'm not sure how to respond to his poetic utterance. I mutter my thanks and leave the queue. I'm disappointed in myself. I've revered the creativity of this man for nearly fifty years, found myself singing his songs to myself on long car journeys, heart-felt anthems to my lost youth, just to end up tongue-tied on my first, and probably last, opportunity to meet him.

It wasn't long after Sensorium's Gregory's Girl tour that Henry announced he was moving to Perpignan in the south of France. On Henry's departure the music of Sensorium disappeared forever into the Celtic twilight.

Throughout my life since around the age of fifteen there has been a fairly continuous stream of bands taking up my spare time. Developing and playing with a group seems to be an essential ingredient in the blueprint of my life, so much so, that without this I would feel there was something missing.

Ailsa attended the Hereford Steiner School. It was at one of the school gatherings that I first heard Chris play. He stood in a corner, a halo of long frizzy hair spiking out from his head as if it were electrically charged, and placed his soprano saxophone gently in his mouth. What came forth was a liquid golden river of phrases, improvised in the moment. Another time Chris was the warm up act for a visiting Bossa Nova band from Bristol, playing locally at a village hall. On this occasion he played tenor saxophone. Again, he played solo, this time improvising eloquently on a John Coltrane tune.

Speaking to him afterwards I felt I had met a kindred spirit. I approached him about forming a band. The desire to be making and developing music in a band context was so strong that I was happy to hang up my saxophone and move on to the piano. Playing jazz piano was a challenging task for me but several years of playing piano at The Angel had prepared me to some extent for that role.

Initially we were a trio, our third member being Manu Song, a gifted musician and percussionist. We called ourselves Big Sky Trio, a name that I feel reflected our eclectic influences of music from around the world. We did some lovely gigs in Bristol and Herefordshire but after a year or so, Manu announced he would have to leave in order to resolve family commitments.

I invited my friend and neighbour Carles to dust down his fretless bass guitar and come to join us. Many moons ago, back in Barcelona, Carles had been promised a chance to go to the jazz course at Berklee College to study under the bass guitar genius, Jaco Pastorius. Tragically, Jaco died of injuries inflicted on him by bouncers at a night club who had misinterpreted his challenging bi-polar behaviour. Carles never got to meet the great man.

Soon after we auditioned and welcomed Pedro as our new drummer and percussionist. It was all coming together nicely.

In 2016 I was diagnosed with prostate cancer. I had surgery to remove my prostate and several adjacent lymph glands, followed by six bouts of chemotherapy. At the end of this treatment my oncologist was concerned about the enlargement of my lymph glands detected in CT scans. I had an investigative biopsy of these nodes taken from my abdomen. Struggling on the phone with the difficulty of imparting more bad news my oncologist told me I had another type of cancer. This one was follicular lymphoma. Another six bouts of chemo then followed which, miraculously, from the outset of very first treatment, took away the uncomfortable swelling in my abdomen. I lost my hair, lost weight and crept around like a ghost of my former self for several months.

Throughout all this, I enjoyed the fantastic support of Julia and my loving daughters.

Meanwhile, the band, in its new quartet configuration, kept playing through this phase of my recovery. We enjoyed each other's playing, rehearsed regularly and picked up opportunities to perform.

One time, chatting with us at the end of a gig, a friend confronted us with the interesting news that we were not the only band going under the name of 'Big Sky.' Another outfit, specialising in Country and Western music were also using the name. What is more, they also came from South

Wales. The possibility of both bands showing up at a booking was not a distant possibility. Finding a new name for the band suddenly became a priority.

Obtaining just the right nuance for a band's name is a tricky business. I remember regretting the choice of the name 'Cado Belle' for my seventies band which might have suggested to some people that we specialised in Louisiana-style Cajun music. After too much time wasted at our rehearsals, debating lists of suggestions, we eventually decide on Nuadha Quartet, this in spite of Carles' protestations that the name 'Nuadha' had dodgy overtones in his native Catalan. 'If we ever play in Barcelona' he warned, 'we should expect audiences of 'S and M' devotees. We decided to put off worrying about that until we got to Barcelona.

Nuadha was the first High King of ancient Ireland, one of the semi-mythological Tuatha-de danann. Legend has it that he lost his hand in battle, and as he was no longer perfect, he was, by the rules of the day, unfit to reign. Fortunately, he had a new silver hand made for him which, with the help of a bit of magic, was seven years later turned into flesh. Once again, he was able to take over the kingship and ruled for a further twenty years.

I took this legend to heart. After making my way through two major cancer events and coming out relatively unscathed I felt that I, like Nuadha, had been given a second chance. Shortly after our re-naming, Nuadha Quartet recorded its first album, Cabin Tales, an eclectic blend of tunes penned by Chris and myself.

My daughter, Ailsa, has worked hard to establish herself as a music artist. She began her song writing career eight years ago, using an acoustic cello as her accompaniment. The acoustic instrument was replaced for a while with an electric cello before she made the transition to her Fender Mustang electric bass guitar. How different the life of a young musician is these days. There are deals to be signed with record labels but they are like gold-dust and often the musician's artistic control is compromised. Even before the pandemic, gigs were poorly paid and hard to come by. It is well-nigh impossible to generate income by releasing a single or album as people prefer to go to a streaming service rather than buy a song online. Young musicians have to cover a wide range of skills in order to get ahead; having to be adept at home recording, blogging, promoting, video editing, not to mention the ability to craft interesting songs.

What a difference to when I was starting out as a professional musician in my early twenties. The climate for musicians back then was definitely more favourable with so many opportunities coming to my door.

Now mired and bogged down during a global pandemic most musicians are stuck at home. Some are enterprising enough to record and video themselves, sharing their latest musical offerings on the various social media platforms. Most would agree that this is a poor substitute for the experience of performing to an audience that is present with you, be it in a hall, a lounge bar or a stadium. We, the musicians, long for the day when the seemingly endless lockdowns come to an end and the precious gift of music can once again be shared.

Let us hope we can all turn the page and begin that new chapter very soon.

A friend recently asked that very frank question; what does music mean to me? I mulled it over for a few days. There are so many responses that music can bring out and I have to assume that what it means to me is common to all people who are sensitive to music. When it comes down to it, it can be expressed simply; music is the catalyst for us to experience an expanded sense of being alive.

Sometime in the late nineties I bought myself a ticket to hear the famous Brazilian musician, Egberto Gismonte, who was playing in Bristol at St George's. I remember that during the first half of the performance Egberto played guitar with a string quartet for which he had scored beautiful and elegant parts. In the second half of the performance, I took myself up to the crowded gallery at the back of the hall. There were no available seats but I didn't mind standing at the back. The excitement was palpable, this being a rare privilege for Bristolians to witness a world class musician in peak form. Egberto came back on stage and sat himself at the St George's grand piano. After flicking his mane of hair behind his shoulders his hands began to dance across the piano keys. Whilst he was master of a unique and personal guitar style Egberto was first and foremost a pianist. I've always loved Brazilian music with its rich blend of harmonic movement and subtle rhythm and not only did Egberto have his country's musical legacies well under his belt he delivered them with the finesse and expertise of a concert pianist. My position at the top of the gallery must have been some kind of acoustic 'sweet spot' as the music rose up to us from the stage, perfectly balanced. Standing behind everyone in the audience made it easy to drop my natural reserve and I soon found myself so intoxicated by the music that I had no choice but to dance. As wave after wave of neat and nimble soloing poured forth from Egberto's fertile imagination I was responding in the way that Brazilian music ultimately wants us to, its patterns and rhythms re-awakening the pure joy of existence.

A few weeks ago, I found myself in hospital again. A CT scan revealed that my lymphoma had returned and they kept me in for a few days' observation. Discomfort and the noisiness of the ward meant that getting a decent sleep was a challenge. A few weeks before I had been scrolling through my phone and rediscovered Andreas Wollenveider, a Swiss harpist who had impressed me back in the eighties. Lying in my hospital bed I decided to play the video of a 'mini concert' (mini concert 6) of his which I particularly liked. Since the 1980s Andreas has evolved into a benign avuncular character but who has lost none of the precision and beauty in the playing, he had back in his youth.

The electro-harp shimmers as he produces a lullaby tune in a minor key. There is something in the yearning quality of the melody that begins to open me up to a vulnerable state. The tightness created by the worry and discomfort of my hospital stay begins to release and I am melting, my throat choked up and behind my eyes there is a sudden build-up of tears to be shed. Hidden by the ward curtains and with my headphones on I now have my own private melt-down. The fear that this latest cancer event is setting me up for my final journey takes hold in the rush of thoughts. The harp music, however, counteracts the gloom with its sunshine notes. Images rush before my eyes; my daughters, Julia, friends, family; everyone I have ever loved, a fast-moving video of the important people in my life. As the music plays on, I manage to banish the dark thoughts and cherish the good ones.

In my twenties, I would play my favourite music either on a record or an audio-cassette player. Sometimes, for me the music I was listening to would be so special, so beautiful, that if I suddenly had to go out half way through the piece, I would find the emotional wrench of not hearing the piece in its entirety very difficult. To walk away from the music seemed disrespectful. It felt to me that music had a message, a vibration that, even though it was just a recording emanating from my little cassette machine, the world needed to hear it. So, as I left my room, I would let the music play on, convinced that even without anyone listening, it was making this world a better place.

Music. Our species song. Long may it play on.